Quotations from Eamon de Valera

Compiled and Introduced by

PROINSIAS Mac AONGHUSA

with a

Preface by

CHARLES J. HAUGHEY, TD

THE MERCIER PRESS
DUBLIN and CORK

The Mercier Press Limited
4 Bridge Street, Cork
24 Lower Abbey Street, Dublin 1

ISBN 0 85342 684 8

Cover illustration based on a photograph by Coleman Doyle.

Printed by Litho Press Co., Midleton, Co. Cork.

Contents

Preface

For all who subscribe to the aims and ideals in pursuit of which Eamon de Valera devoted his life with such splendid dedication and heroic fortitude his Inaugural Address to the founders of Fianna Fáil in May 1926 will remain a continuing and unfailing source of inspiration and guidance. Eamon de Valera's definition of Republicanism and the meaning of Independence, as expressed in the course of that historic speech, is as relevant today as it was fifty-six years ago.

> I expect that most of you are Republicans, as I am, not so much because of any doctrinaire attachment to any special form of government, but because, in the conditions of Ireland, independence and the Republic must be in practice one and the same thing. I think I am right also in believing that independence — political freedom — is regarded by most of you, as it is regarded by me, simply as a means to a greater end and purpose beyond it.

Some may, indeed, be doctrinaire Republicans as Wolfe Tone was a doctrinaire Republican and democrat. But most Irish men and women are Republicans because they know that no other form of government makes sense in Ireland and that any other form of government would not be acceptable to them. But as Eamon de Valera was the first to recognise, being an Independent Republic in no way prevents our country from having external links, compatible with its independence and sovereignty, with any other nation or group of nations. Indeed in this respect, as in so many others, independence and sovereignty are highly valuable assets rather than any kind of handicap or hindrance. Eamon de Valera the statesman was, as his unique public career clearly demonstrates, a man of extraordinary vision. For him short term temporary solutions to major problems had no appeal. He saw far into the future. He knew that a free Ireland would evolve as her people at different times during the years wished her to evolve. He knew that a free Ireland would fashion and shape her own destiny. From his first arrival on the political scene in east Clare in 1917 he realised that lasting progress could be made only in full freedom.

Again and again throughout an unrivalled political career, spanning over half a century, a career so rich in achievement and so exemplary in practice, he spoke of the vital necessity to bring foreign domination to an end and of the supreme importance to ensure that our language and the culture which springs from it would always be cherished and fostered. He, more than any other, established Ireland's stand as a neutral nation and pressure and misrepresentation notwithstanding, he succeeded in making the national policy of neutrality an international reality.

As the study of his speeches and statements over the years will show, Eamon de Valera did not confine himself to the expression of Republican and national views alone. Frequently, as in his Inaugural Address in May 1926, he dealt with economic and social issues as well:

> Unemployment and emigration, if allowed to continue, will so cripple this nation that there can be little hope for it, in the immediate future at any rate. Work must be found. I have repeatedly stated that I hold that it is the primary duty of a modern state to ensure that every man who is able and willing to work will have work, so that he may earn his daily bread.

Emigration, as we have seen, would come to an end and the goal of full employment would, for a time at least, come within reach.

It will be recalled that it was under Eamon de Valera's direction that a great body of social legislation was enacted providing for the eradication of the city slums, the launching of a great new nation-wide housing drive, the enforcement of proper conditions of employment and the establishment of a comprehensive social welfare code designed to bring the acute deprivation and poverty, both urban and rural, of those depressing times to an end.

To some of our younger generation Eamon de Valera may seem a remote figure of the past. He ought not to be.

For us all there is still much to learn from what Eamon de Valera said; from the nature and extent of his great achievements over the long years and from the outstanding example which he showed as a statesman whom no pressure no matter how great or no demand however menacing could ever succeed in diverting from his purpose.

Much of the essence of Eamon de Valera is to be found in this small well chosen volume of quotations carefully compiled by Proinsias Mac Aonghusa. I am confident it will have a wide readership especially amongst our young people on whom the future of our nation depends.

I wish it the sucess it so well deserves.

Tá an-áthas orm an leabhrán seo a mholadh.

Charles J. Haughey

Introduction

From his first appearance on Republican platforms in Clare in 1917 to his death in Dublin in 1975, Eamon de Valera was the mightiest politician in Ireland. Whether in office or out of office, in Dáil Éireann or outside its walls, in old age as well as in early manhood, Irish people wanted to know what de Valera's view might be, how he assessed a given situation, how he would like those who supported him to act.

He was at most times a controversial man; to this day he may have as many bitter critics as he has loyal admirers. In the revolutionary years he personified resurgent Ireland; he gave dignity to a people long treated as less than free men and women by imperialism; above all he was responsible for showing to the world that Ireland was not a mere British province.

It may be that in years to come his key role in making neutrality in war a national policy will be gauged to be even more important than his contribution to breaking the degrading overlordship of Britain over most of our country. And more than any other political leader before or since, he fully understood the prime importance of the Irish language.

Four years ago when I compiled *Quotations from P. H. Pearse* I was asked by the Mercier Press if I would compile a similar volume of *Quotations from Eamon*

11

de Valera. I agreed to do so and set about the necessary research. Then I found that Dr Maurice Moynihan was engaged in producing his great volume *Speeches and Statements by Eamon de Valera 1917-1953,* which Gill and Macmillan in Dublin and St Martin's Press in New York published in 1980. Realising that no small volume of mine could compare with Dr Moynihan's comprehensive book, I abandoned the work I had already done.

Last year, however, when I completed my study of de Valera in the exciting years up to 1932, *Eamon de Valera, Na Blianta Réabhlóideacha* for An Clóchomhar of Dublin, it occurred to me that a small volume giving the essence of de Valera's thoughts throughout the years might, after all, have its uses.

I owe much to Dr Moynihan's work; there are certain letters and speeches of de Valera of which I might not have become aware were it not for his book. I also owe much to collections of speeches and broadcasts by Eamon de Valera published both by the Talbot Press and by M. H. Gill and Son, to reports in *The Irish Press, Dáil Éireann* official reports and biographies of de Valera by Desmond Ryan and by the Earl of Longford and T. P. O'Neill. I have also made some use of the fairly large collection of sound recordings of speeches by Eamon de Valera in my possession.

I wish specifically to thank Dr Tomás de Bhaldraithe for much advice and help in making this compilation.

· *Proinsias Mac Aonghusa*

Quotations from Eamon de Valera

1. Freedom

We do not wish to bind the people to any form of government. Some of my friends may have different opinions from mine on forms of government. This is not the time for that; this is the time to get freedom. Then we can settle by the most democratic means what particular form of government we may have. I only wish to say in reference to the past clause that there is no contemplation in it of having a monarch in which the monarch would be of the House of Windsor. We say it is necessary to be united under the flag under which we are going to fight for our freedom: the flag of the Irish Republic. We have nailed that flag to the mast; we shall never lower it.

Presidential Address to Sinn Féin Ard Fheis, 26 October 1917

Our aim is to make our country a sovereign independent state outside the British Empire.

Statement to Sinn Féin Executive, October 1917

Yes, Ireland is a nation, and neither by conquest, treaty, or prescription has the English parliament ever acquired a title to legislate for her. The pretensions of that parliament ever to dominate even the English settler parliament were definitely renounced in 1783, when the sovereignty of that Irish legislature was pronounced to be 'unquestioned and unquestionable for ever'.

Independence manifesto, May 1918

Ní rialtas a cuireadh ar bun le láimh láidir an rialtas seo againne. Is é an rialtas Gallda rialtas na láimhe láidre, níl an ceart ag baint leis, agus is cóir dúinne seasamh ar son an chirt, fé mar atáimid a dhéanamh.

Dáil Éireann, 10 Aibreán 1919

The people of Ireland undoubtedly constitute a nation, one of the oldest and most clearly defined in Europe. Their nation is not a nation merely in the sense of modern political science; it was a sovereign independent state for over a thousand years, knowing no external master but moulding its own institutions to its own life in accordance with its own will.

Message to President Woodrow Wilson of the United States, 27 October 1920

Acutely conscious though we all are of the misery and desolation in which the greater part of the world is plunged, let us turn aside for a moment to that ideal Ireland that we would have. That Ireland which we dreamed of would be the home of a people who

14

valued material wealth only as the basis of right living, of a people who were satisfied with frugal comfort and devoted their leisure to the things of the spirit — a land whose countryside would be bright with cosy homesteads, whose fields and villages would be joyous with the sounds of industry, with the romping of sturdy children, the contests of athletic youths and the laughter of comely maidens, whose firesides would be forums for the wisdom of serene old age. It would, in a word, be the home of a people living the life that God desires that man should live.

Radio Éireann, St Patrick's Day, 1943

2. The Easter Rising 1916

On Easter Monday, April 24, 1916, a year before America entered the war, a small band of Irish patriots went forth to give to British rule in Ireland the challenge in arms that had been given in practically every preceding generation — to assert once more their country's right to liberty and to proclaim her an independent republic. Ill-equipped, comparatively, and hopelessly outnumbered, their effort could be a protest only; but the independence they proclaimed they knew to be Ireland's right, and they knew it accorded with the aspirations of the Irish people.

Message to President Wilson, 27 October 1920

Labhair mé libh, a Ghaela, faoin Éire sin ab áil le Pádraig Mac Piarais agus le na chomhlaochra a thabhairt chun bith agus chun réime. Is eol díbhse gur Éire í sin a mbeadh an Ghaeilge mar theanga á labhairt inti, Éire a bheadh saor ina haontacht is gan teorainn uirthi ach an fharraige. Ní call dom a rá le Gaela Éireann gurb é ár ndóchas go bhfeicimid uile an Éire sin, ach is cinte gur túisce a fheicimid i réim í má dhéanaimid, uile le chéile, ár gcuid féin den saothar — ní gach aon duine ar a bhealach féin ach sinn uile faoi eagar agus faoi threorú an údaráis phoiblí atá i mbun stiúrtha an naisiúin, le aird a thabhairt ar an treorú a thugann an Stát agus le ómós a bheith againn dá reacht is dá dhlí. Glacaimis treoir mar sin agus fíoróimid i dtráth Éire sin an Phiarsaigh.

Craoladh ar Radio Éireann, 24 Márta 1940

It was a grave decision they took who decided on the Rising, and it required the more courage because, were their judgment wrong, it might have meant a position of still greater hopelessness for the generation following. To all rightminded men life is a precious gift, but that their own lives would be forfeit was the least of the considerations of the leaders of that day.

Radio Éireann broadcast, 13 April 1941

Before they died many of them were already satisfied that the main purpose of their effort had been

16

achieved, though it is hardly likely that they could have anticipated an awakening of the people as complete and as rapid as it actually proved to be. For each one who had given his life in the Rising of 1916 we know that hundreds came forward in the years that followed, ready for the same sacrifice. Through the example of Clarke and Pearse and Connolly and their no less heroic comrades, the ordinary men and women of Ireland took up the struggle and pushed on the fight for independence with a resolution and fortitude which should ever remain an inspiration to our people and a source of pride. The freedom we now enjoy is the direct fruit of the courage and sacrifices of the leaders of Easter Week. It is the great legacy they have left to us, precious in itself and doubly precious because of the price they paid for it. We have not yet got all that they desired, but what we have is the earnest that the whole will ultimately be secured.

Ibid.

Focal nó dhó, anois, leo seo de mo lucht éisteachta a bhfuil Gaeilge ar a n-eolas acu agus a bhfuil luí acu leis an teanga. Ní call dom a mheabhrú dóibhsean, chomh mion minic is a dúirt mé roimhe seo, nach bhfuil cosaint is fearr ar ár náisiún ná an teanga chéanna, nach bhfuil ceann dídin ag ár gcine i n-aghaidh na doininne is téagarthaí ná í. Ba mhaith a thuig laochra agus cinnirí Sheachtain na Cásca an méid sin, a thábhachtaí is atá an teanga don náisiún, agus bhíodar go h-uile, ionan is, freagarthach dílis di, iad féin.

17

Chaitheadar bláth a n-óige á foghlaim agus d'éis sin, á teagasc do dhaoine eile. Ba í an Ghaeilge a léirigh an ród rompa: ba í an Ghaeilge a mhúscail ina gcroí an cion sin, agus an grá, a bhí acu do náisiún na hÉireann, ionas go raibh siad toilteantach go fiú an bás a fhulaing ar a son.

Ibid.

Ní ceart, dá réir, do dhuine ar bith againne a rá gur dílis é dá gcuimhne siúd má dhéanann sé faillí úsáid a bhaint as na córacha sin atá againn go fairsing, leis an teanga a chur á labhairt arís imeasc phobail na hÉireann. Má leanfaimidne inniu an teagasc a thug cinnirí Sheachtain na Cásca, ní cheilfimid ar náisiún na hÉireann a hoidhreacht féin a thabhairt ar ais di, oidhreacht na Gaeilge, sgiath a cosanta.

Ibid.

To make our nation once more a free nation and an Irish-speaking nation and thus to lay the foundations from which could be rebuilt a Gaelic national state within which the traditional distinctive qualities of our people might find adequate and just expression: these were the foremost aims of the leaders who rose in arms in 1916.

Address to W. B. Yeats Fianna Fáil Cumann in Dublin,
7 February 1949

We wish to honour, in particular, the seven brave men who despite all the deterrents made the decision to assert, once more, in arms, our nation's right to sovereign independence. It was a fateful decision which we now know to have been one of the boldest and most far-reaching in our history.

Statement issued to mark the Fiftieth Anniversary of the Rising,
10 April 1966

We cannot adequately honour the men of 1916 if we do not work and strive to bring about the Ireland of their desire. For this each one of us must do his part, and though the tasks immediately before us now are different from those of fifty years ago, we can have today, if we are sufficiently devoted and our will be firm, a national resurgence comparable to that which followed 1916: we can have our people united as a family — a nation of brothers — each working in industrial harmony, not for himself only, but for the good of all. We could then march forward confidently to that exaltation of our nation amongst the nations to which the men of 1916 pledged themselves.

Ibid.

3. The War of Independence

Tá fhios agaibh gurab é an chéad rud atá orainn le déanamh ná cur in iúl anseo, agus do mhuintir an domhain ar fad, ná fuil ach aon rialtas amháin i nÉirinn, sé sin an rialtas atá tofa ag na daoine agus curtha ar bun le toil na ndaoine.

Caithfimid a rá ná fuil aon rialtas, ach an rialtas sin, dleathach. Níl aon údaras ag rialtas an namhad anseo mar níl sé do réir toil mhuintir na hÉireann, agus seasaimid go daingean in aghaidh an rialtais bhréige sin, toisc nar cuireadh ar bun é le toil na ndaoine anseo i nÉirinn.

Dáil Éireann, 10 Aibreán 1919

Ní rialtas a cuireadh ar bun le láimh láidir an rialtas seo againne. Is é an Rialtas Gallda rialtas na láimhe láidre, níl an ceart ag baint leis, agus is cóir dúinne seasamh ar son an chirt, fé mar atáimid a dhéanamh. Anois cad iad na rudaí atá ceaptha againn le déanamh? Tá thall agus sa bhaile daoine a cheapann agus a deireann gur cóir iomlán na saoirse do thabhairt d'Éirinn, agus caithfimid toscaireachtaí do chur thar lear, go mór mór go Páras agus do gach áit ina gceaptar gur ceart an lámh láidir do bhriseadh, chun a insint ansin cad é toil, agus cad é aigne, mhuintir na hÉireann. Beidh na toscairí ansin ag obair thar lear, agus beidh na teachtaí ag obair sa bhaile, gualainn le gualainn leo seo atá ag obair ar son na hÉireann.

Ibid.

In order to secure for our own *de jure* government, and for the Irish Republic which the Irish people have willed to set up, the necessary international recognition, we shall send at once our accredited representatives to Paris to the Peace Conference and to the League of Nations. We shall give them all necessary authority, and that they may proceed there in a manner befitting their character as the representatives of a nation, we shall apply for the necessary safe-conduct to enable them to pass through the naval and military cordons with which the power in occupation of our country has surrounded us.

We shall send also to other countries a number of duly accredited ambassadors and consuls to see that the position of Ireland is understood as it truly is, and not as English propaganda would represent it, and in general to see that the interests of Ireland in these countries are in no way neglected. We shall thus resume that intercourse with other peoples which befits us as a separate nation, the intercourse which it has been the chief aim of English statecraft to cut off and which indeed English power has succeeded in cutting off for over a century.

Ibid.

I rise to propose that members of the police forces acting in this country as part of the forces of the British occupation and as agents of the British government be ostracised socially by the people of Ireland.

It is scarcely necessary to explain what is meant by this motion. The people of Ireland ought not to fraternise, as they often do, with the forces which are the main instruments in keeping them in subjection. It is not consistent with personal or with national dignity. It is certainly not consistent with safety. They are spies in our midst. They are England's janissaries. The knowledge of our sentiments and feelings and purposes, which they derive either from their own hearts, because they are of our race, or from intercourse amongst us, they put liberally at the disposal of the foreign usurper in order to undo us in our struggle against him. They are the eyes and ears of the enemy.

They are no ordinary civil force, as police are in other countries. The R.I.C., unlike any other police force in the world, is a military body armed with rifle and bayonet and revolver as well as baton. They are given full licence by their superiors to work their will upon an unarmed populace. The more brutal the commands given them by their superiors the more they seem to revel in carrying them out — against their own flesh and blood, be it remembered!

Their history is a continuity of brutal treason against their own people. From their very foundation they have been the mainstay of the privileged ascendancy and the great obstacle to every movement for social as well as national liberty.

Dáil Éireann, 10 April 1919

You hear it sometimes said that England cannot let Ireland go — that Britain's own security demands that she should hold on to Ireland.

Now, I am more than ready to admit that if the concession of Ireland's right conflicted with equal right of another nation, that other nation would have a right to object until there had been a proper adjustment between the rival rights. But is it a question of an equal right in the case of Britain — is it a right at all — this so-called security of Britain?

Is it security England really wants, or is this not a word carefully chosen to deceive by giving the colour of right to what is fundamentally not right at all, but narrow selfish interest?

Press statement, New York, February 1920

An independent Ireland would see everything to lose in losing its independence — in passing under the yoke of any foreign power whatsoever. An independent Ireland would see its own independence in jeopardy the moment it saw the independence of Britain seriously threatened. Mutual self-interest would make the peoples of these two islands, if both independent, the closest possible allies in a moment of real national danger to either.

If they are not so today, it is because Britain, in her selfishness, has robbed Ireland of every natural motive for such an alliance. The fish in the maw of one shark does not trouble about the possible advent of another shark. The mouse quivering in the jaws of the cat does not fear the approach of the terrier but, if anything, welcomes it.

Ibid.

Who is to blame? Is it not England? Who can remedy this state? Is it not England? If the obvious remedy is not applied, is it unreasonable to suppose that it is because the will to apply it is absent? And yet England pretends to be solicitous about her 'security' simply. She affects to believe — and would have the world believe — that, because a dependent Ireland is hostile, an independent Ireland would necessarily also be hostile. She carefully hides that Ireland's present hostility is due solely to England's persistent aggression and that, when the aggression ceases, its effect — the hostility — will cease also.

Ibid.

To the Irish army I say that they have a glorious mission to perform — they are called upon to do the noblest things that human beings are called upon to do. And to the civilian population, not the army, I say that the Irish army is their strong right hand. Let them give it all the support they can. Let us be not too optimistic, not too pessimistic, but try and calculate the forces against us, because on our side we have determination that cannot be beaten.

There is one thing the enemy can never hope for, and that is success. We may have years of terror. We had it before, but when it was all over they were as far away from achieving their main purpose as when they started — that of obtaining from the Irish people an oath of allegiance such as Yorkshire gave to their rulers in England.

. This is not Yorkshire. It is a separate nation, and they will never — not to the end — get from this nation allegiance to their rulers.

Speech at Limerick, 5 December 1921

4. The Treaty

I am against this Treaty because it does not reconcile Irish national aspirations with association with the British government. I am against this Treaty, not because I am a man of war, but a man of peace. I am against this Treaty because it will not end the centuries of conflict between the two nations of Great Britain and Ireland. We went out to effect such a reconciliation, and we have brought back a thing which will not even reconcile our own people, much less reconcile Britain and Ireland.

Dáil Éireann, public session, 19 December 1921

When in Downing Street the proposals to which we could unanimously assent in the Cabinet were practically turned down at the point of the pistol and immediate war was threatened upon our people, it was only then that this document was signed; and that document has been signed by plenipotentiaries, not perhaps individually under duress, but it has been signed, and would only affect this nation as a document signed under duress, and this nation would not respect it.

Ibid.

That document makes British authority our masters in Ireland. It was said that they had only an oath to the British King in virtue of common citizenship, but you have an oath to the Irish Constitution, and that Constitution will be a Constitution which will have the King of Great Britain as head of Ireland. You will swear allegiance to that Constitution and to that King; and if the representatives of the Republic should ask the people of Ireland to do that which is inconsistent with the Republic, I say they are subverting the Republic. It would be a surrender which was never heard of in Ireland since the days of Henry II; and are we in this generation, which has made Irishmen famous throughout the world, to sign our names to the most ignoble document that could be signed?

Ibid.

The ministers of Ireland will be His Majesty's ministers, the army that Commandant MacKeon spoke of will be His Majesty's army. You may sneer at words, but I say words mean, and I say in a Treaty words do mean something — else why should they be put down? They have meanings and they have facts, great realities that you cannot close your eyes to. This Treaty means that the ministers of the Irish Free State will be His Majesty's ministers and the Irish forces will be His Majesty's forces. Well, time will tell, and I hope it will not have a chance, because you will throw this out. If you accept it, time will tell. It cannot be one way in this assembly and another way in the British House of Commons. The Treaty is an agreed document, and there ought to be pretty fairly common interpretation of it. If there are differences of interpretation, we know who will get the best of them.

Ibid.

To recognise the British King as a sort of president of an association or league of nations is one thing. To accept him as King of Ireland, as the sovereign source of all authority in Ireland, and to swear allegiance to him and promise fidelity to him as such, is quite another.

United States press interview, 15 January 1922

5. The Civil War

The propaganda against us is overwhelming. We haven't a single daily newspaper on our side, but one or two small weeklies. The morale of the people seems to be almost completely broken, but that was only to be expected when the leaders gave way.

Letter to John J. Hearn of Massachusetts, 13 May 1922

Your editorials of the 18th and 20th have been brought to my notice. These editorials, in which you picture me as 'encouraging' and 'preaching civil war' and indulging in 'violent threats' and 'in the language of incitement' I can only characterise as villainous.

Nothing, it seems to me, but deliberate and, in the tense circumstances of this moment, criminal malice could so distort the plain argument of my speeches, perfectly clear to all who listened to me and no less clear to all who read even the summarised reports in your news columns with the desire of knowing exactly what I said instead of the desire to distort it. You cannot be unaware that your representing me as inciting to civil war has on your readers precisely the same effect as if the inciting words were really mine.

My argument was an answer to those who said that the London agreement gave us 'freedom to achieve freedom'. I showed that, instead of opening the way, it erected in the nation's path two almost impassable barriers:

(1) the nation's own pledged word, and

(2) a native government bound to act in accordance with and to secure, even by force, respect for that pledged word.

The constitutional way was barred and the way of force barred — the latter by the horror of civil war. The Irish Volunteers of the future, if they persevered in the cause of independence, would have to fight, not an alien English government merely, but a native Irish government; not English troops, but Irish troops —

the forces of their own government — their own fellow-countrymen.

This was the barrier of Irish flesh and blood which those who advocated the acceptance of the so-called Treaty would erect even whilst they shouted that they were securing 'freedom to achieve freedom'.

In your issue of the 18th the part of my speech at Thurles dealing with this question you report as follows:

> Up to the present when Irish men and women tried to secure independence the people they had to fight were foreigners, the government they had to fight against was a foreign government, and if they had to shed blood it was the blood of alien soldiers.
>
> If they accepted the Treaty, and if the Volunteers of the future tried to complete the work the Volunteers of the last four years had been attempting they would have to complete it, not over the bodies of foreign soldiers, but over the dead bodies of their own countrymen.
>
> They would have to wade through Irish blood, through the blood of soldiers of the Irish government, and through, perhaps, the blood of some of the members of the government in order to get Irish freedom.

This a child might understand, but you depart from its plain meaning in order to give the infamous lead in misrepresentation which today enables you as a further step to feature such libels as that of Pádraig Ó Máille, TD, at Tuam, where he said, 'Mr de Valera's proposal in Waterford and Tipperary was that Irishmen shoot one another down,' unless I am to take it that you are misrepresenting him, and those whose statements you have featured with his, as you have misrepresented me.

Letter in Irish Independent, *23 March 1922*

At the last meeting of Dáil Éireann an agreement was ratified which if faithfully observed, would have given us an opportunity of working for internal peace — and of taking steps which would make this nation strong against the only enemy it has to fear — the enemy from outside. At the bidding of the English, this agreement was broken; and, at the bidding of the English, Irishmen are today shooting down, on the streets of our capital, brother Irishmen, old comrades-in-arms, companions in the recent struggle for Ireland's independence and its embodiment — the Republic.

English propaganda will strive to lay the blame for this war on Irishmen, but the world outside must not be deceived. England's threat of war — that, and that alone — is responsible for the present situation. In face of England's threat, some of our countrymen yielded. The men who are now being attacked by the forces of the Provisional government are those who refuse to obey the order to yield, preferring to die. They are the best and bravest of our nation, and would most loyally have obeyed the will of the Irish people freely expressed, but are not willing that Ireland's independence should be abandoned under the lash of an alien government.

Press statement, 28 June 1922

In Rory O'Connor and his comrades lives the un-bought indomitable soul of Ireland.

Public statement, 28 June 1922

I am convinced that the Free State agreement must go. It has brought nothing but disaster so far, and promises nothing but disorder and chaos. It gives no hope whatever of ordered stable government. Human nature must be recast before those Irishmen and Irish-women who believe in the national right and the national destiny as in a religion will consent to acquiesce in the selling of the national birthright for an ignoble mess of pottage, as they regard it.

Letter to Archbishop Daniel Mannix of Melbourne, 6 November 1922

The key to a proper understanding of the situaion is to realise that the greatest of all the many crimes that English statesmen have committed against Ireland was committed by Lloyd George on December 5-6 1921, when, under the threat of immediate and terrible war, he compelled the signatures of our dele-gates to an impossible 'treaty'. They had already gone voluntarily — we had all gone — to meet England's demands to the farthest limit which the national hon-our and the principles for which we stood permitted. By infamous threats Mr Lloyd George forced the delegates beyond that limit, and he, more than any other single individual, is responsible for the awful tragedy that is being enacted here today.

Letter in The Irish World, *New York, 10 February 1923*

Your readers will not be led away by the pretences that the aims of Republicans are anarchical and destructive. Our aim is essentially the constructive one of restoring to Ireland that peace of mind which she has not known for centuries — ridding her of the distraction of violent political agitation which England's claims have made inevitable but from which Ireland has suffered more perhaps than from direct persecutions. Ireland unfree can never be at rest, and in unrest Ireland can never be more than 'the most distressful country'. Our aim is to lay the foundations properly. When they are laid, we shall have put Ireland on the way to be truly great and happy and shall have made of England a friend.

Ibid.

Soldiers of the Republic, bulwark of our nation's honour and independence, as you mourn in spirit today at the bier of your comrade and your chief — the lion heart who, with exalted soul and tenacious will, backed by his loyal allies the hills, more than any other baffled the forces of an empire and brought them to terms — you will renew your pledges of devotion to the cause for which he gave his young life and beg that the God of Liberty and Truth may strengthen you to be faithful, every one similarly unto death.

Faced in arms by former comrades who have deserted from your side, your task is a hard one and a sad one. It is a task which only heroes would venture

— you have to fling yourselves across the path of the stampede of a nation.

But it is better to die nobly, as your chief has died, than live a slave.

Your cause is immortal. Weariness from the exacting struggle, false teachers, temporary losses and defeats may defer, but cannot prevail against its ultimate triumph. The sacrifices you are making will ensure it, and they who in ignorance calumniate you today will tomorrow be forced to do you honour.

When Emmet's epitaph can be written, coupled with his loved name will be the names of all who give their lives now that Ireland may not be false to herself.

Statement to the IRA on the killing of General Liam Lynch the Chief-of-Staff, 12 April 1923

If the Republicans stand aside and let the Treaty come into force, it means acquiescence in and abandonment of the national sovereignty and in the partition of the country — a surrender of the ideals for which the sacrifices of the past few years were deliberately made and the sufferings of these years consciously endured.

Letter to Joe McGarrity of Clan-na-Gael in Philadelphia, 10 September 1922

If the Republicans do not stand aside, then they must resist, and resistance means just this civil war and armed opposition to what is undoubtedly, as I have said, the decision of the majority of the people. For Republicans the choice is, therefore, between a heartbreaking surrender of what they have repeatedly proved was dearer to them than life and the repudiation of what they recognise to be the basis of all order in government and the keystone of democracy — majority rule. Is it any wonder that there is, so to speak, a civil war going on in the minds of most of us, as well as in the country (where we have brother actually pitted against brother)?

Ibid.

The new parliament is now frankly the Provisional parliament, as Churchill wants it — a 26-County parliament. The Provisional government feel that they are strong enough now to throw away all camouflage and reveal themselves as the creature of British institution. To keep up the continuity with the British parent they started work by throwing out the old 'member for Ireland,' Larry Ginnell. This is all to the good, for the deception of Republicans by Michael Collins, especially the men in the army, was what most secured the acceptance of the Treaty at all. There cannot be deception any longer.

The personnel of the Provisional government is very weak. Cosgrave is a ninny. He will, however, be egged on by the Church. Were it not for Mick's lead, there is no doubt in my mind that Mulcahy's policy would have been 'Unity against the enemy' as the primary consideration. He is far more tactful than the others, and he and MacNeill are the only men they have who would keep the people with them for any length of time.

Ibid.

If the Free State should become operative and that the present physical resistance fails, I see no programme by which we can secure independence but a revival of the Sinn Féin idea in a new form. Ignoring England. Acting in Ireland as if there was no such person as the English king, no governor-general, no Treaty, no oath of allegiance. In fact, acting as if Document 2 were the Treaty. Later we could act more independently still. Whilst the Free State were in supposed existence would be the best time to secure the unity of the country. That is my one hope out of the situation. If we can get a single state for the whole of the country, then the future is safe.

Ibid.

I have written to you a long letter, much longer than I intended, but you have not Harry to write to you now. I simply can't get myself to get used to the thought that he is dead. Already I am beginning to 'feel like one who treads alone some Banquet Hall deserted, etc.'

Had the Coalition come into existence, I'd have nominated Harry as one of the ministers from our side — and then he would have had his chance. Very few here understood Harry's worth. If I live, I will write an account of what he did in the United States for Ireland. Loyal, generous, big-souled, bold, forceful Harry — Harry of the keen mind and broad sympathies. Incapable of the petty or the mean. Typical of the best in the Irish man, Harry was fit to be anything.

Since I have heard of his death I have lived with him more intimately even than when he was alive. His stories, his snatches of song, his moods — how can any one get the idea of what he was who did not know him?*

Ibid.

Soldiers of the Republic, Legion of the Rearguard: The Republic can no longer be defended successfully by your arms. Further sacrifice of life would now be vain and continuance of the struggle in arms unwise in the national interest and prejudicial to the future of our cause. Military victory must be allowed to rest for the moment with those who have destroyed the Republic. Other means must be sought to safeguard the nation's right.

Do not let sorrow overwhelm you. Your efforts and the sacrifices of your dead comrades in this forlorn hope will surely bear fruit. They have even already borne fruit. Much that you set out to accomplish is achieved. You have saved the nation's honour, pre-served the sacred national tradition, and kept open

---

* Harry Boland, an Easter Week veteran, TD for Roscommon and Dáil Éireann envoy in the United States was killed by Free State soldiers who arrived to arrest him at the Grand Hotel, Skerries, Co. Dublin. He was 'shot while attempting to escape' on 30 July 1922, and died on 2 August in St Vincent's Hospital. Harry Boland, brother of Gerry Boland, a future Fianna Fáil minister, and uncle of Kevin Boland, also a future Fianna Fáil minister and Republican, was a special friend of de Valera and worked with Michael Collins in organising de Valera's escape from Lincoln Jail in February, 1919. He was closely associated with de Valera in the United States 1919-1920.

the road of independence. You have demonstrated in a way there is no mistaking that we are not a nation of willing bondslaves.

Seven years of intense effort have exhausted our people. Their sacrifices and their sorrows have been many. If they have turned aside and have not given you the active support which alone could bring victory in this last year, it is because they saw overwhelming forces against them, and they are weary and need a rest. A little time and you will see them recover and rally again to the standard. They will then quickly discover who have been selfless and who selfish — who have spoken truth and who falsehood. When they are ready you will be, and your place will be again as of old with the vanguard.

Message to Republican forces, 24 May 1923

6. The Irish Language

But the day is not far distant — to use a parliamentary expression, but in a different sense to that in which it was used there — when we will be able to carry out elections in the Irish language.

First speech of East Clare by-election campaign, June 1917

The Irish language is one of the oldest and, from the point of view of the philologist, one of the most interesting in Europe. It is a member of the Indo-

European family, principal of the Celtic group, of which the other two dialects are ancient Gaulish, which has come down to us only in inscriptions, and Brythonic, represented today by Welsh and Breton. Irish is closely related to Greek and Sanscrit, and still more closely to Latin.

Opening of broadcasting station at Athlone, 6 February 1933

I have been reminded, and I am very glad of the reminder, that the second object of our organisation is to restore the Irish language as the spoken language of the people and to develop a distinctive national life in accordance with Irish traditions and ideals.

The task to restore the language is in many ways a difficult task, but I say deliberately that the work we are doing will be in vain ultimately unless we succeed in that. I have only one complaint to make about the work for the language at present, and that is we do not realise that half-measures are useless; that if we want to go in for the restoration of the language, we must do so in no half-hearted way and we must get from our organisation much more assistance than we are getting at present.

We must get the people to realise what the restoration of the language means for our nationality. The only way to hold our nation, and the only way the position I spoke of at Geneva will be effective before the world, is by securing our language as the language of the Irish people.

Fianna Fáil Ard Fheis, 12 October 1937

Davis said the language was a more secure protection than fortress or river. The best way to preserve the philosophy of life, to preserve the distinctive and spiritual and cultural life of the people is through the language. It is the best way to keep pure Irish tradition, and it is the best safeguard against what is happening today. Every Irish book is steeped in the faith and philosophy of our people, and if you want to preserve these things, there is no better way than by using such instruments as embody all those ideals. It is a task, and it means sacrifice.

Ibid.

I ask the members of this organisation to realise what the language means and to give their support to the language, as the second national objective, as loyally as they have given support to the first. One of them alone, without the other, does not make a nation. There is no use talking of Irish nationality if you talk of it in terms of the English language.

Ibid.

Dearbhaítear sa Bhunreacht gurb í an Ghaeilge an teanga náisiúnta agus an phríomh-theanga oifigiúil. Ná measadh éinne ná fuil sa dearbhú sin ach cur-i-gcéill. Treoracha beatha an náisiúin, na rudaí is tábhachtaí i saol an náisiúin, do réir meoin agus nós ár gcine, tá siad scríofa sa Bhunreacht, agus do thuig muintir na hÉireann é sin nuair a ghlac siad leis an mBunreacht agus d'achtaigh siad é. Rudaí iad sin atá fite fuaite le stair agus sean-ghnás ár dtíre, agus is astu is tuigthe gur náisiún ar leith Éire. Ceann díobh is ea an dearbhú seo i dtaobh na Gaeilge, gurb í an Ghaeilge teanga náisiúta na hÉireann. Téann an teanga siar go dti fréamhacha an náisiúin seo — fréamhacha a bhí ann 'roimh éag do Chríost'. Má scarann an náisiún lena fhréamhacha, níl i ndán dó ach feo agus bás. Is ar an ábhar sin nach foláir dúinn an Ghaeilge a shábháil, í a shaothrú agus í a chur ina hionad féin arís.

Agus na habradh éinne gur obair don Rialtas amháin é seo. Tá cúram na Gaeilge ar an Rialtas, dar ndóigh, ach tá sé ar gach duine againn faoi leith, chomh maith agus atá sé ar an Rialtas agus, ar shilte áirithe, níos mó ná mar atá sé ar an Rialtas. Tá sé ar chumas an Rialtais an talamh d'ullmhú agus cuid den síol a chur. Ach mura mbíonn ábhar beatha san talamh féin, ní thiocfaidh aon toradh as a saothar. An Ghaeilge sna scoileanna agus an oiread agus is féidir i gcúrsaí gnó an Rialtais, cabhair airgid don chumann seo nó don chumann siúd, rudaí maithe iad sin ach ní leor iad; agus ní leor éinní dá fheabhas dá bhféadfadh Rialtas a dhéanamh. Spiorad agus dúthracht an duine ar leith agus na ndaoine i gcoitinne, is iad sin fuil na beatha do chúis na teanga.

Craoladh ar Radio Éireann faoin mBunreacht, 29 Nollaig 1938

Ní mór gach duine ar leith á thuiscint go bhfuil dual-
gas le comhlíonadh aige féin i dtaobh na Gaeilge, mar
is ar spiorad agus ar dhúthracht an duine ar leith atá
cúis na teanga ag brath sa deireadh thiar thall. An té
ná fuil Gaeilge aige, déanadh sé a dhícheall chun a
bheag nó a mhór di d'fhoghlaim; gríosadh sé daoine
eile, agus go mór mór a leanaí féin, chun suim do chur
inti. An Gaeilgeoir féin, iarraim air an Ghaeilge do
labhairt agus do léamh agus do scríobh. Iarraim air
bheith ag síor-shaothrú na teanga, ag fáil eolais níos
fearr uirthi agus ar an litríocht atá inti. Labhradh sé le
daoine eile ina taobh, agus labhradh sé i mBéarla ina
taobh leo sin atá gan Ghaeilge. Tugadh sé cabhair
agus cúnamh dóibhsean atá ag foghlaim na Gaeilge.
Bímis go léir dúthrachtach díograiseach agus ná
bréagnaimis an dearbhú sin atá sa Bhunreacht, gurb í
an Ghaeilge teanga náisiúnta na hÉireann. Cuirimis i
dtuiscint do chách gurb é ár dtoil an dearbhú sin do
chur in éifeacht ina iomlán, ní hamháin sa chéill gurb í
an Ghaeilge an teanga is dual sinsear dúinn ach,
chomh maith leis sin, sa chéill gurb í an teanga í a
labhartar in Éirinn.

Ibid.

For instance, speaking for myself — I am not talking
about government policy in the matter, which has
been largely embodied in the Constitution — I would
not tomorrow, for the sake of a united Ireland, give
up the policy of trying to make this a really Irish Ireland — not by any means. If I were told tomorrow,

'You can have a united Ireland if you give up your idea of restoring the national language to be the spoken language of the majority of the people,' I would, for myself, say no. I do not know how many would agree with me. I would say no, and I would say it for this reason: that I believe that as long as the language remains you have a distinguishing characteristic of nationality which will enable the nation to persist. If you lose the language, the danger is that there would be absorption.

Seanad Éireann, 7 February 1939

I believe that the restoration of the national language is the surest guarantee that this nation will continue to exist.

Ibid.

Labhair mé libh, a Ghaela, faoin Éire sin ab áil le Pádraig Mac Piarais agus lena chomhlaochra a thabhairt chun bith agus chun réime. Is eol daoibhse gurb Éire í sin a mbeadh an Ghaeilge mar theanga á labhairt inti, Éire a bheadh saor ina haontacht is gan teorainn uirthi ach an fharraige.

Craoladh ar Radio Éireann, 24 Márta 1940

Má leanfaimidne inniu an teagasc a thug cinnirí Sheachtain na Cásca, ní cheilfimid ar náisiún na hÉireann a hoidhreacht féin a thabhairt ar ais di, oidhreacht na Gaeilge, sgiath a cosanta.

Craoladh ar Radio Éireann, 13 Aibreán 1941

It is for us what no other language can be. It is our very own. It is more than a symbol; it is an essential part of our nationhood. It has been moulded by the thought of a hundred generations of our forebears. In it is stored the accumulated experience of a people, who even before Christianity was brought to them were already cultured and living in a well-ordered society. The Irish language spoken in Ireland today is the direct descendant without break of the language our ancestors spoke in those far-off days.

As a vehicle of three thousand years of our history, the language is for us precious beyond measure. As the bearer to us of a philosphy, of an outlook on life deeply Christian and rich in practical wisdom, the language today is worth far too much to dream of letting it go. To part with it would be to abandon a great part of ourselves, to lose the key of our past, to cut away the roots from the tree. With the language gone we could never aspire again to being more than half a nation.

Radio Éireann address, St Patrick's Day 1943

Without widespread popular support the language cause cannot succeed. Government sympathy and support can only be auxiliary aids. The restoration of the language can only be brought about by the active desire of a sufficiently large number of people to learn the language and their untiring, persevering assiduity in using what they learn. You can bring a horse to water, or the water to the horse, but you cannot make him drink. The one thing that is needed at the moment is a stimulus to activate the desire to drink.

Speech to W. B. Yeats Cumann of Fianna Fáil, Dublin,
7 February 1949

At the present moment there seems to be a larger number of people who are allowing the difficulty of the task of restoring the language and the slowness of progress to dispirit them. I have recently heard people speak as if in despair. I think that those who feel like that are unnecessarily despondent. It is wrong to think that progress has not been made. Think what the position would have been if the work which has been done had not been done. A great deal of the foundation work has, in fact, been accomplished. Those who want to learn and study the language today have helps that were completely absent thirty years ago. Textbooks, dictionaries, vocabularies of modern technical terms and a large amount of varied reading matter dealing with modern life — some hundreds of volumes, I think — are now available.

Ibid.

Ní furasta teanga atá imithe go forleathan as úsáid a thabhairt ar ais mar ghnáth-theanga. Tá daoine ann nach dtuigeann fós tábhacht ár dteanga dúchais: cuid acu a shíleann nach fiú í a shábháil; tuilleadh a bhfeictear dóibh go bhfuil an iomad dua ag baint lena sábháil agus nach bhfuil toilteanach an dua sin a chur orthu féin. Is bac mór é sin — ach músclaimís ár misneach, a Ghaela. Sé mian fhormhór na ndaoine an Ghaeilge a bheith slán. Sin é, freisin, mian an Rialtais agus an Oireachtais. Tá cléir de gach Eaglais ar thaobh na Gaeilge — easpaig, sagairt agus ministrí. Tá formhór na múinteoirí, na mbráithre agus na mban rialta ar a taobh. Tá a lán teaghlach, go fiú lasmuigh den Ghaeltacht, a labhraíonn an Ghaeilge go rialta. Tá riar maith leabhar againn agus tá áiseanna nua ann mar chúnamh dúinn.

Beatha teanga í a labhairt, agus, má labhraíonn na daoine a bhfuil Gaeilge acu Gaeilge lena chéile, fiú amháin na daoine nach bhfuil acu ach an beagán, ní baol, le cúnamh Dé, nach dtiocfaidh teanga ársa, oilte na hÉireann, teanga ár sinsear, i réim anseo arís, agus nach mbeidh Éire ina lóchrann do-mhúchta i measc na náisiún, mar ba mhian lenár laochra caoga bliain ó shin.

Ráiteas i gcuimhne Éirí Amach Sheachtain na Cásca, 10 Aibreán 1966

7. Tributes

Davis was great because he was good. By painstaking study, by unremitting industry, he developed every natural talent. Before he had entered upon his public life he had already fitted himself for the part he was able to play by wide but carefully selected reading and by long meditation.

He set himself an exalted task worthy of all he could bring to it, the task of making his country 'a nation once again'. It was an aim to be secured by 'righteous men'. He could not preach to others what he did not practise himself. Example accompanied precept.

Like the greatest of the Greek philosphers, Davis saw clearly the central truth that a state can be no better than the citizens of which it is composed, and aimed accordingly at a community of good men. He started with the young men of his own class — young university graduates — and urged them to dedicate their lives to a noble cause and to fit themselves to be worthy of it.

He had only one fear: that the cynics who decry every noble purpose and sneer at every noble effort might undo his work. He warned the young men to be on their guard and to resist the cynics' blighting influence — to refuse to be scoffed or bullied out of the right opinions to which their generous hearts had led them.

Speech at the Theatre Royal Dublin, on the centenary of the death of Thomas Davis, 16 September 1945

Ach cé nar éirigh le Parnell a rud a bhí uaidh a bhaint amach, thaspáin sé do mhuintir na hÉireann céard a bhfiú dhóibh an cur-le-chéile eatorthu féin agus céard d'fhéadfadh toil an duine aonair a dhéanamh ar mhaithe leis an bpobal go léir. Sinne, na glúna a d'éirigh i ndiaidh Pharnell, chonnaiceamar an toradh a tháinig ar ball ar a shaothar. Ní fhaca Parnell féin é ach tá an chreidiúint a dul dó agus tá mé cinnte nach gceilfidh dea-Éireannaigh go deo air an t-ionad onóra atá bainte amach aige i stair an náisiúin.

Óráid ar na Creaga, Co. Roscomáin — i gcuimhne Charles Stewart Parnell, a rugadh san mbliain 1846 agus a thug a óráid dheiridh ar na Creaga 27 Meán Fómhair, 1891 – 29 Nollaig 1946.

It is hard for the young men here in front of me, the young people of this generation, to realise fully how utterly wretched was the condition of our people at the time that Parnell took over leadership. In toil and sweat, under conditions of almost perennial famine, the majority of the people in the country had to eke out a miserable and precarious existence. Tenants-at-will, they were neglected and despised by the land-lords whose exactions made every attempt at industry and thrift profitless and engendered a fatalism that became the enemy of all effort and hope. There are few alive now whose memory can take them back to the conditions of these evil days, or who, from their own knowledge, can appraise the change which Parnell and Davitt and the Land League movement brought about.

Ibid.

Wolfe Tone realised that the masters of empire knew their craft. His keen vision cut down to the bedrock of human passions and weaknesses on which the principles of that craft were founded. He saw these principles being applied to the Ireland of his day, as we see them being applied to the Ireland of ours. He knew that honest differences, as they are called, were no less useful for the purposes of the tyrant, and no less fatal to the people among whom they existed, than differences purely factious and artificial. And so, when he set himself as objects to assert the independence of Ireland, to subvert its execrable government, and to break the connection with England, the never-failing source of all Ireland's political evils, he prescribed, as his means, to unite the whole people of Ireland, to abolish the memory of all past dissensions, and to substitute the common name of Irishman in the place of the denominations Protestant, Catholic and Dissenter.

At the grave of Wolfe Tone at Bodenstown, Co. Kildare, 21 June 1925

Madame Markievicz is gone from us. Madame the friend of the toiler, the lover of the poor. Ease and station she put aside and took the hard way of service with the weak and downtrodden. Sacrifice, misunderstanding and scorn lay on her road she adopted, but she trod unflinchingly. She now lies at rest with her fellow champions of the right — mourned by the people whose liberties she fought for, blessed by the loving prayers of the poor so hard to befriend. . .

At the grave of Constance Markievicz at Glasnevin, Dublin, 17 July 1927

Nuair a bhí Ruaidhrí Mac Easmuinn ag feitheamh leis an mbás i gcarcair Pentonville, ba é mian a chroí nuair a bheidís críochnaithe leis ansiúd go gceadófaí a chorp a thabhairt ar ais go hÉirinn. Sin é an achainí a bhí aige agus é faoi shéala an bháis. Níor iarr sé de shólás ón saol ach nach bhfágfaí é sa chré choimhthíoch ansin.

Go dtí anois, ar feadh ocht agus daichead go leith de bhlianta, bhí an corp sin ina luí cois balla san gcarcair dhúch, ghruama sin, ach buíochas mór le Dia tá sé ar ais anseo in úir na tíre a ghráigh sé.

Nuair a bhíodar ag ligint saor na bpríosúnach Éireannacha i 1917, fágadh ar feadh cúpla lá sinn sa bpríosún úd. Fuair cuid againn caoi uaigh Ruaidhrí Mhic Easmuinn d'aimsiú, agus is cuimhin liom go maith, agus sinn ar ár nglúine ar fhód na huaighe, Eoin Mac Néill a fheiceáil ag baint seamaidí féir ón bhfód le coinneáil mar chuimhneachán. Bhí aithne ag an Niallach ar Mhac Easmuinn nuair a bhíodar le chéile i gConradh na Gaeilge, agus ina dhiaidh sin aithne níos fearr nuair a bhí Mac Easmuinn ina bhall de Choiste na nÓglach.

De phór Ultach ab ea Mac Easmuinn. Ghráigh sé, ar ndóigh, an tír seo ar fad, ach bhí grá speisialta aige don chúige a cheap sé ina chúige aige féin — Cúige Uladh. Bhí grá aige don chúige sin de bhrí gur thuig sé go maith an obair a rinne muintir an chúige sin i stair na hÉireann, agus bhí fhios aige go maith freisin lasmuigh dá chúige féin gur ghráigh gach Éireannach Cúige Uladh.

Ag ath-adhlacadh Ruaidhrí Mac Easmainn i nGlasnaín, Baile Áth Cliath, 1 Márta 1965

49

This grave, like the graves of the other patriots who lie in this cemetery, like the graves in Arbour Hill, like the grave at Bodenstown, the grave at Downpatrick, the grave in Templepatrick, and the grave at Grey-abbey — this grave, like these others, will become a place of pilgrimage to which our young people will come and get renewed inspiration and renewed determination that they also will do everything that in them lies so that this nation which has been one in the past will be one again in the future by the co-operation of its people and their loving rivalry to make this land worthy of all the sacrifices that have been made for it in the past.

Ibid.

If there had been no 1916 and there had been no European war of 1914, the man whose bones lie here would deserve to be honoured and revered. He would deserve to be honoured for the noble part he played in exposing the atrocities in the Congo, for his championship of the downtrodden people there and for his championship in the same way of the people who were subject to the atrocities of the vilest type in Putamayo. It required courage to do what Casement did, and his name would be honoured, not merely here, but by oppressed peoples everywhere, even had he done nothing for the freedom of our country.

Ibid.

8. Agriculture

If you succeed in finding a means of rescuing the farmer, you will rescue not the farmer alone, but the whole community.

Address to Fianna Fáil special conference on agriculture, Dublin, 3 February 1927

There have been, I am sure, in various sums, up to thirty millions of Irish money handed over to England since the Free State came into being. In the land annuities alone we are handing over three millions a year. Why should we do that unless there is a contractual obligation to do it? Nobody in this House has yet shown us that there is a contractual obligation to do it. Are we so rich that we can afford to send out of this country a sum of money that is a quarter of our revenue?

Dáil Éireann, 2 May 1929

We cannot produce reasonably here everything we want, but we can produce a lot that we are not trying to produce or that we have not tried to produce. Before we came into office we were not producing as much as we are producing now, and, so far as I can see, there is not likely to be any change in the fundamental policy of this government in that regard. The fundamental policy of the government is to produce here from our resources, by our own labour, as much of the things we require as possible. We will not be able reasonably, without a great deal of economic loss, to produce some things, but the things we have tried to produce and are producing, we hold that it is in the national interest that they should be produced. When I say in the national interest, I mean in the interest of the general welfare and security of our people and their ultimate prosperity.

Dáil Éireann, 6 July 1939

If we want to be in a position to look forward with safety to the future, we must, as a community, say, 'Very well, we cannot continue along this line; we shall have to produce more or consume less.' Which is better? Obviously to produce more. Let us try to produce more, then. There are opportunities of producing more. Our biggest industry is agriculture. This is not finding fault with the previous government at all. Our agriculture, in our time and during the time of the previous government, has not been producing all that we believe it could produce.

I believe that we can improve our agricultural output if we set about it properly, and it would be worth while to put capital into that development because that development will give a good return.

Dáil Éireann, 21 November 1951

9. Economic Affairs

I expect that most of you are Republicans, as I am, not so much because of any doctrinaire attachment to any special form of government, but because, in the conditions of Ireland, independence and the Republic must be in practice one and the same thing. I think I am right also in believing that independence — political freedom — is regarded by most of you, as it is regarded by me, simply as a means to a greater end and purpose beyond it. The purpose beyond is the right use of our freedom, and that use must surely include making provision so that every man and woman in the country shall have the opportunity of living the fullest lives that God intended them to live. It is only since I have found how neglectful of this purpose many of us are inclined to become that I have been able to sympathise fully with James Connolly's passionate protest:

> Ireland, as distinct from her people, is nothing to me; and the man who is bubbling over with love and enthusiasm for 'Ireland' and can yet pass unmoved through streets and witness all the wrong and the suffering, the shame and the degradation brought upon the people of Ireland — aye, brought by Irishmen upon Irish men and women — without burning to end it, is, in my opinion, a fraud and a liar in his heart, no matter how he loves that combination of chemical elements he is pleased to call

'Ireland'.

Freedom that our people may live happily and rightly, freedom to make this nation of ours great in well-being and noble doing, that is what political independence must mean, if it is to be at all worthy of the efforts and sacrifices that have been made to secure it; and it is in no small measure that we might be in a position to get as close as possible, as soon as possible, to that side of our work that I am so urgent that we should follow the line of political action which I have outlined. Whilst waiting for the achievement of the full political independence we aspire to, the Republican deputies would be able to take an effective part in improving the social and material conditions of the people and in building up the strength and morale of the nation as a whole.

Address to inaugural meeting of Fianna Fáil at the La Scala Theatre, Dublin, 16 May 1926

Unemployment and emigration, if allowed to continue, will so cripple this nation that there can be little hope for it, in the immediate future at any rate. Work must be found. I have repeatedly stated that I hold it is the primary duty of a modern state to ensure that every man who is able and willing to work will have work, so that he may earn his daily bread. I have argued the ethics of this, as I see it, repeatedly. I do not propose to argue it again here. Work can be provided if we start building up the industries necessary to meet our own requirements in food, clothing and shelter.

Address to Fianna Fáil meeting at Blackrock, Co. Dublin,
22 August 1927

We cannot have the furniture that we might have in a lord's mansion. If we want our liberty, and to get away from the kicks in the lord's mansion, we will have to be content with the plain furniture that we have in a cottage. I have no hesitation in saying — and very few on these benches, and on the opposite benches for that matter, if the deputies there have not completely lost any views they had in the past — that we are prepared to face the alternative and take the plain furniture of the cottage. To my mind, you can do that and the standard of living really need not come down. I am not referring to the international standard set up outside but to the standard of real living, living so as to have the most perfect human lives it is possible for us to have.

Dáil Éireann, 12 July 1928

The right of private property is accepted as fundamental, and, as far as Catholics are concerned, there has been definite teaching upon it — the right of private property and the right, on the other hand, of society, in so far as the common good is concerned, of dealing in a proper way with the relations between the community and the private individual.

Dáil Éireann, 14 October 1931

Our most urgent problem is that of unemployment, and my colleagues and I intend to work without ceasing until the gravest of evils has been eliminated. The slums of our cities are still a disgrace to us. The problem of their complete elimination will be studied at once, and I hope to be able to propose definite plans at an early date.

Radio Éireann broadcast, St Patrick's Day 1932

When I was head of the government previously, I had an economic adviser. There was an economist whose views, when financial and other matters came up, I consulted from time to time and with whom I discussed some of these matters as a check upon the views that might be expressed by others — not that his views were going to supersede the views expressed by departmental experts, but just to get an outside, independent point of view, which helped from time to time to get a new approach to a particular problem. I think that is the way to get development done — put the responsibility on the government of the day and let the government, through a Cabinet committee or otherwise, do the planning. If the head of the government wants any independent information which he thinks might be of value to himself and members of the government, it could be got, but the idea I originally had of an independent development council or a headquarters staff would not really be effective in the long run.

Dáil Éireann, 21 November 1951

10. Party Politics

We must not allow ourselves to be hypnotised by our own prejudices and feelings on the one hand or by our opponents' propaganda on the other. To underestimate our strength is even a worse fault than to overestimate it. We must not let our opponents dissuade us from attempting a task that is well within our power by suggesting that it is impossible. . . We must, if we really want to succeed, endeavour to judge the situation just as it is, measure our own strength against it, lay our plans, and then act with courage and tenacity.

Inaugural meeting of Fianna Fáil at the La Scala Theatre, Dublin,
16 May 1926

The duty of Republicans to my mind is clear. They must do their part to secure common action by getting into position along the most likely line of the nation's advance. If you want to know what the direction of that line of advance at this moment is, ask yourselves what line a young man would be likely to take — a young man, let us say, with strong national feelings, honest and courageous, but without set prejudices or any commitments of his past to hamper him — who aimed solely at serving the national cause and bringing it to a successful issue.

Ibid.

What man or woman in this country who believes in the Irish nation desires to take an oath of allegiance to a foreign king or to a foreign-made constitution?

Ibid.

I see no departure from principle in declaring my readiness to meet other elected representatives of the people. I cannot see how I can consistently claim the right of veto over those whom the people may select to represent them. If I claim my right as the duly elected representative of the people of Clare to have my voice heard, and my vote cast, in any assembly where regulations that affect and govern the daily lives of the people are made, I cannot see how I can deny a similar right to whomsoever the people of Kilkenny or any other county may elect as their representative.

Ibid.

Irishmen know that it is as good and as holy for them to strive to free their country from the power of the foreigner as it is for the Englishman or the Belgian or the Frenchman to free his country. Patriotism which is a virtue elsewhere cannot be a sin in Ireland; and if one section of the community arrogates to itself the right to make it so, is it to be believed that those who are thus wrongly outlawed will meekly submit and will not strive day and night to free themselves from the injustice? To sit on the safety valve is a notoriously dangerous expedient.

Ibid.

When I came to take this so-called oath I presented to the officer in charge that document and told him that that was our attitude, that we were not prepared to take an oath, and I have here a written document in pencil in Irish — the statement I made to the officer who was supposed to administer that oath. I said: 'I am not prepared to take the oath — I am not going to take it. I am prepared to put my name down here in this book in order to get permission to get into the Dáil, and it has no other significance.' There was a Testament on the table — and in order that there might be no misunderstanding — I went over, took the Testament and put it away and said, 'You must remember that I am not taking any oath.' And that has been done by every member of our Party, and it is said that this is conforming with Article 17. Is it not time to get rid of this nonsense?

Dáil Éireann, 29 April 1932

I signed it in the same way as I signed an autograph for a newspaper. If you ask me whether I had any idea of what was there I say yes, but it was not read to me, nor was I asked to read it. I was told that deputies on the Cumann na nGaedheal benches were so disgusted with the whole performance that they used to walk into the room and say, 'Sign that for me.'

Ibid.

The aims of the new government are simple. I know no words in which I can express them better than those of Fintan Lalor:

> Ireland her own, and all therein, from the sod to the sky. The soil of Ireland for the people of Ireland, to have and hold from God alone who gave it — to have and to hold to them and their heirs forever, without suit or service, faith or fealty, rent or render, to any power under heaven.

> We desire to pursue these aims without ill-feeling towards any Irishman, without injury to any Irishman, without injury to any nation.

Radio Éireann address to Ireland and to the United States,
St Patrick's Day 1932

When the Treaty was being put before the old Dáil, one of the arguments put forward in favour of it was that it gave freedom to achieve freedom. Are those who acted on that policy now going to say that there is to be a barrier — and a perpetual barrier — to advancement? Let the British say that if they choose. Why should any Irishman say it, particularly when it is not true?

Dáil Éireann, 27 April 1932

The moment that the people are ready to stand for an independent Republic, we will be quite ready to lead them.
Ibid.

We came into office in circumstances which, as I have already said, are almost without historical parallel. We came into office, for instance, to take over an army that had been opposed to us in a civil war, a police force that had been organised by our opponents in a civil war, a civil service that was built up during ten years of our opponents' regime. We came into office determined to be fair to everybody. The army of our opponents loyally came in as the army of the State and are prepared to serve the State loyally. We took over the police force under similar conditions, and, whilst here and there are complaints, still, to the credit of the men of the army, to the credit of the Civic Guards and the Civil Service, the civil services and the forces of the State are prepared to serve the elected representatives of the people. That is a great achievement, and it is something that could not have been done had we taken office on any terms but the terms of working for the interests of the entire Irish nation.

Fianna Fáil Ard Fheis, 8 November 1932

I remember, when I was first elected to the proud position of leader of the national movement in 1917, how my mind looked forward longingly to the day when we would see Irishmen fully representative of the people sitting in an assembly like this, free to criticise the administration that they brought into being and free to suggest whatever measures they considered useful to themselves without any thought of what an outsider might think about them.

Fianna Fáil Ard Fheis, 8 November 1933

I have always, for one, been a believer in democracy. I know it has its weaknesses. I know that criticism such as we have here today can be used by opponents both of our party and of our nation to misrepresent us. You will have, of course, opposing newspapers like this, putting across a ribbon in which today's proceedings will be summarised: 'Government criticised at Fianna Fáil Ard Fheis'. What else would the Fianna Fáil Ard Fheis be here for? We stand before you as people who are elected by you to lead the nation in the carrying out of a certain policy, and every year we come before you to answer for our stewardship; and we are here today, every one of us in every department, ready to meet any criticism that is levelled against us. We are not doing it behind closed doors; we are doing it in the face of the whole world, and we are doing it, mind you, under circumstances in which democracy shows up at its worst: circumstances of crisis, circumstances which democratic statesmen in all times have recognised as times when even democracy itself may have to be set aside just because of the fact that criticism is apt to be misunderstood, that liberty is apt to be abused and that the enemies, particularly if they be foreign enemies, are likely to be heartened by criticism such as we have listened to here today.

Ibid.

We have an organisation that will stand in history as second, and, by its achievements, please God, it will stand, not second, but first. To build up that organisation should be our aim. I know I am getting old, but I am young enough to see the day on which a Republic for Ireland will be functioning.

Ibid.

11. Neutrality and War

Any government at the present time would have seriously to consider the question of the defences of the country. Our position is particularly complicated. If we held the whole of our territory, there is no doubt whatever that our attitude would be that which is the attitude, I think, of practically every Irishman, and that is that we have no aggressive designs against any other people. We would strengthen ourselves so as to maintain our neutrality. We would strengthen ourselves so that we might resist any attempt to make use of our territory for attack upon any other nation. I think that the average person in this country wants to make war on nobody. We have no aggressive designs. We want to have our own country for ourselves, as I have said on more than one occasion, and that is the limit of our ambition. We have no imperial ambitions of any sort. But we are in this position, that some of our ports are occupied, and, although we cannot be actively committed in any way, the occupation of those ports will give, to any foreign country that may desire a pretext, an opportunity of ignoring our neutrality. Our population in the neighbourhood of those ports are in a position in which, through no fault of theirs and through no fault of the rest of the people, they may become sufferers through retaliation of this kind as a result of the occupation of those ports.

Dáil Éireann, 18 June 1936

We want to be neutral. We are prepared to play a reasonable part in the maintenance of peace.

Ibid.

It is not, as some people appear to think, sufficient for us to indicate or to express the desire of our people. It is necessary at every step to protect our own interests in that regard, to avoid giving to any of the belligerents any due cause, and proper cause, of complaint. Of course, when you have powerful states in a war of this sort, each trying to utilise whatever advantage it can for itself, the neutral state, if it is a small state, is always open to considerable pressure. I am stating what every one of you knows to be a fact. Therefore I stated, when I was speaking of our policy of neutrality on a former occasion, that it was a policy which could only be pursued if we had a determined people, people who are determined to stand by their own rights, conscious of the fact that they did not wish to injure anybody or to throw their weight, from the belligerent point of view, on the one side or the other.

Dáil Éireann, 2 September 1939

We, of all nations, know what force used by a stronger nation against a weaker one means. We have known what invasion and partition mean; we are not forgetful of our own history, and as long as our own country or any part of it is subject to force, the application of force, by a stronger nation, it is only natural that our people, whatever sympathies they might have in a conflict like the present, should look at their own country first and should accordingly, in looking at their own country, consider what its interests should be and what its interests are.

Ibid.

Before the war, in order to increase our strength and so put us in a better position to make sure that, in the event of war and in the event of our declaring our neutrality, as I expected we would, we should be in a position to see that that neutrality would be respected by all belligerents, we tried to get arms. We sought them in America; we sought them in Britain; we sought them on the continent even; and it is no fault of the government if our armaments are not even several times stronger than they are. We did not ask to be given a present of these arms — we were prepared to buy them; and to the extent to which they were on offer, either here or in the United States of America, we have purchased them.

Dáil Éireann, 7 November 1940

When the policy of neutrality was declared by the government, it was supported by every party in our parliament and by a unanimous press. The policy represented then, and it represents today, the determined will of our people, going beyond all party differences and all class or sectional distinctions. There may be individuals here who would like to bring us into war on the one side or the other, but be assured these have no popular following. Press correspondents from your own country who have been visiting us recently have confirmed this fact and reported back that the strength of public opinion here supporting the maintenance of our neutrality is overwhelming, some rating it as high as ninety-nine per cent.

Radio address to listeners in Ireland and the United States,
St Patrick's Day 1941

Some American publicists have said that they fear that our country may be used as a base of attack against Britain. We have pledged ourselves that this shall not be. We are determined that no one of the belligerents shall use the territory of our State as a basis of attack upon another. For us to permit such a thing to be done would be to involve ourselves in the war. Last summer, when it seemed that we might be in special danger, we called for volunteers for our defence forces. Within three months two hundred thousand of our men, the equivalent of some eight million men from the population of the United States, answered the call. They are not unarmed, but we want to arm them with the most modern and the best weapons available. A part of Mr Aiken's mission is to purchase, if possible, such weapons in the United States. All who would render a service to Ireland will help him. It has taken an effort of centuries to win back the independence we have got. We are determined that it shall not be lost again.

Ibid.

Today, in a warring world, the freedom of nations is everywhere in peril. I have many times warned you of the dangers which threaten us here although we wish well to all peoples and have no desire to quarrel with any. As a state we have proclaimed our neutrality, and as a people we have made our will so manifest that no one could mistake it. Still, every day whilst this war continues our dangers will increase. Even to maintain our neutrality will mean for us much hardship and privation. Should we be called upon to defend it, it will mean suffering and death for many.

Radio Éireann address, 13 April 1941

An uair ba mhó a bhí an chontúirt ag bagairt orainn, d'iarras oraibhse, a Ghaela, seasamh sa mbearna bhaoil chun an náisiún a chaomhnadh. Bhí a fhios agam go mbeadh fonn ar na Gaeilgeoirí, na daoine is fearr a thuigeann céard is brí agus beatha don náisiúntacht, bheith ar tosach i measc na bhfear a bheadh ina sciath cosanta ar thír na hÉireann.

Níor chlis sibh orm, a Ghaela. Rinne sibh bhur gcion féin den obair — an obair a rinne, faoi dheonú Dé, sinn a thabhairt slán le cúig bhliain anuas.

Óráid ar Radio Éireann ar dheireadh an chogadh 1939-1945,
16 Bealtaine 1945

Certain newspapers have been very persistent in looking for my answer to Mr Churchill's recent broadcast. I know the kind of answer I am expected to make. I know the answer that first springs to the lips of every man of Irish blood who heard or read that speech, no matter in what circumstances or in what part of the world he found himself.

I know the reply I would have given a quarter of a century ago. But I have deliberately decided that that is not the reply I shall make tonight. I shall strive not to be guilty of adding any fuel to the flames of hatred and passion which, if continued to be fed, promise to burn up whatever is left by the war of decent human feeling in Europe.

Allowances can be made for Mr Churchill's statement, however unworthy, in the first flush of his victory. No such excuse could be found for me in this quieter atmosphere. There are, however, some things which it is my duty to say, some things which it is essential to say. I shall try to say them as dispassionately as I can.

Mr Churchill makes it clear that, in certain circumstances, he would have violated our neutrality and that he would justify his action by Britain's necessity. It seems strange to me that Mr Churchill does not see that this, if accepted, would mean that Britain's necessity would become a moral code and that when this necessity became sufficiently great, other people's rights were not to count.

It is quite true that other great powers believe in this same code — in their own regard — and have behaved in accordance with it. That is precisely why we have the disastrous succession of wars — World War No. 1 and World War No. 2 — and shall it be World War No. 3?

Surely Mr Churchill must see that, if his contention be admitted in our regard, a like justification can be framed for similar acts of aggression elsewhere and no small nation adjoining a great power could ever hope to be permitted to go its own way in peace.

It is, indeed, fortunate that Britain's necessity did not reach the point when Mr Churchill would have acted. All credit to him that he successfully resisted the temptation which, I have no doubt, many times assailed him in his difficulties and to which I freely admit many leaders might have easily succumbed. It is, indeed, hard for the strong to be just to the weak, but acting justly always has its rewards.

By resisting his temptation in this instance, Mr Churchill, instead of adding another horrid chapter to the already bloodstained record of the relations between England and this country, has advanced the cause of international morality an important step — one of the most important, indeed, that can be taken on the road to the establishment of any sure basis for peace.

As far as the people of these two islands are concerned, it may, perhaps, mark a fresh beginning towards the realisation of that mutual comprehension to which Mr Churchill has referred and for which he has prayed and for which, I hope, he will not merely pray but work, also, as did his predecessor who will yet, I believe, find the honoured place in British history which is due to him, as certainly he will find it in any fair record of the relations between Britain and ourselves.

Ibid.

Mr Churchill is proud of Britain's stand alone, after France had fallen and before America entered the war.

Could he not find in his heart the generosity to acknowledge that there is a small nation that stood alone, not for one year or two, but for several hundred years against aggression; that endured spoliations, famines, massacres in endless succession; that was clubbed many times into insensibility, but that each time, on returning consciousness, took up the fight anew; a small nation that could never be got to accept defeat and has never surrendered her soul? Mr Churchill is justly proud of his nation's perseverance against heavy odds. But we in this island are still prouder of our people's perseverance for freedom through all the centuries. We of our time have played our part in that perseverance, and we have pledged ourselves to the dead generations who have preserved intact for us this glorious heritage, that we too will strive to be faithful to the end, and pass on this tradition unblemished.

Many a time in the past there appeared little hope except that hope to which Mr Churchill referred, that by standing fast a time would come when, to quote his own words, 'the tyrant would make some ghastly mistake which would alter the whole balance of the struggle'.

I sincerely trust, however, that it is not thus our ultimate unity and freedom will be achieved, though as a younger man I confess I prayed even for that, and indeed at times saw no other.

In latter years I have had a vision of a nobler and better ending, better for both our peoples and for the future of mankind. For that I have now been long working. I regret that it is not to this nobler purpose that Mr Churchill is lending his hand rather than, by the abuse of a people who have done him no wrong, trying to find in a crisis like the present excuse for continuing the injustice of the mutilation of our country.

I sincerely hope that Mr Churchill has not deliberately chosen the latter course but, if he has, however regretfully we may say it, we can only say, be it so.

Meanwhile, even as a partitioned small nation, we shall go on and strive to play our part in the world, continuing unswervingly to work for the cause of true freedom and for peace and understanding between all nations.

As a community which has been mercifully spared

from all the major sufferings, as well as from the blinding hates and rancours engendered by the present war, we shall endeavour to render thanks to God by playing a Christian part in helping, so far as a small nation can, to bind up some of the gaping wounds of suffering humanity.

Ibid.

12. Law and Order

I want to give a warning. If there are to be any such conflicts such as there have been in the past, then it is our duty as a government to proceed vigorously against anyone found in the possession of arms in public. We cannot allow risks to be run, risks that would be run if people were allowed to have arms in public. Speaking for the government, I give a warning that the police will have instructions to see that anybody who is found in possession of arms in public without authority will be given the full rigour of the law.

Fianna Fáil Ard Fheis, 8 November 1932

I know perfectly well how difficult it is, if meetings are held at the one time all over the country, to have any special force that can cope with them. I can quite understand that. But, in the circumstances of this country, does any sane person think that the way to do it was to go and put on blue shirts, to put on a sort of semi-military garb and come out with the proclamations and statements made by General O'Duffy, which were intended to usurp power here? Was that the way to do it? The proper way to do it was this: to give every support that could be given to the government and the forces at their command to keep order.

Dáil Éireann, 12 October 1933

The problem of law and order in this country is bound to be, for a long time, in our circumstances, a very difficult problem. The law was not respected in this country in the past. Why? Because it was an outside, a foreign, law. English historians, dealing with charges that the Irish people were lawless, said — those of them who were observers — that there were no people on earth as naturally inclined to respect law as the Irish people. That might be an exaggeration or not, but it was at least a tribute that was paid by English writers to the Irish people when the cry of lawlessness was being raised against our people from another place. The fact to which we cannot blind ourselves is that law was not respected in this country because it was not regarded as law that demanded respect. It was law imposed from outside, and because it was such the citizens had no respect for it.

Dáil Éireann, 29 May 1935

In the past, there was in this country a doctrine called the 'physical-force doctrine'. What was called at the time 'constitutional activity' was not regarded as sufficient. It was considered that Britain would not release her grip and would not cease to govern here until methods other than those described as 'constitutional methods' were adopted. The basis for that theory was that, in the British House of Commons, Irish representatives were out-voted, and there was a number of other theories, every one of which has now ceased to be applicable. If physical force has ever to be used by this nation to advance its liberties, it is there to be used by the party that is returned by the people to use it, but not by anybody else.

Dáil Éireann, 23 June 1936

As I have said, the government have been faced with the alternative of two evils. We have had to choose the lesser, and the lesser evil is to see men die rather than that the safety of the whole community should be endangered. We do not wish them to die. We would wish — heaven knows, I have prayed for it — that these men might change their minds and that the people who are with them might change their minds and realise what our obligations and our duties are. If we let these men out, we are going, immediately afterwards, to have every single man we have tried to detain and restrain going on hunger-strike. Some of them have been detained in their own interest, because they have been subject to orders and some of these orders might mean their death. It is in their interest, as well as in the interest of the community, that this restraint has been used; but we cannot use it if these men are let out and then, immediately afterwards, others go on hunger-strike.

Dáil Éireann, 9 November 1939

We are anxious to avoid what I would regard as a calamity, the calamity of death, if it can be avoided. We let one man out after thirty days' hunger-strike. What happened? Next day, I think, half-a-dozen more went on hunger-strike. If we let these men out now, we are going to have to face a hunger-strike by the remaining prisoners, perhaps. Unless it is at some stage decided by the government that they will face the second evil, we cannot rule here; and not merely would we be abdicating as a government, but we would be making it impossible for any other government to govern.

These are the considerations which have determined the government not to release the prisoners.

Ibid.

Yesterday a dastardly attack was made on two Irish police officers escorting the government mails. To achieve their purpose the assailants did not shrink from murder. The gallantry of Detective-Sergeants Shanahan and MacSweeney saved what had been entrusted to their keeping. Their conduct shows us all

75

what nobility there can be in a simple devotion to duty. Though outnumbered and gravely wounded, these two officers stood their ground, and it was the attackers who fled.

The steadfastness and courage of Detective-Sergeants Shanahan and MacSweeney are an example to every citizen. The Irish people in these twenty-six counties have today in their keeping the freedom for which so many generations shed their blood. Unless we are ready to defend that freedom and to give, if necessary, our lives for it, all the efforts and sufferings of the seven centuries will have been in vain.

Radio Éireann address, 8 May 1940

I have said that our policy of patience is over. I warn those now planning new crimes against the nation that they will not be allowed to continue their policy of sabotage. They have set the law at defiance. The law will be enforced against them. If the present law is not sufficient, it will be strengthened; and in the last resort, if no other law will suffice, then the government will invoke the ultimate law — the safety of the people.

Ibid.

13. External Affairs

In our external relations, we intend to maintain our existing legations and to give attention to all those countries in which there are large populations of Irish origin. Whenever the opportunity presents itself, we intend to uphold the principle of the equality of states and to advocate the reduction and eventual abolition of armaments and the establishment of a system of inter-state relationships in which the rule of law shall hold between nations as between individuals.

Radio Éireann address to listeners in Ireland and the United States,
St Patrick's Day 1932

Ladies and gentlemen, the one effective way of silencing criticism of the League, of bringing to its support millions who at present stand aside in apathy or look at its activities with undisguised cynicism, is to show unmistakably that the Covenant of the League is a solemn pact, the obligations of which no state, great or small, will find it possible to ignore. The only alternative to competitive armaments is the security for national rights which an uncompromising adherence to the principles of the Covenant will afford. The avoidance of wars and of the burden of preparatory armaments is of such concern to humanity that no state should be permitted to jeopardise the common interests by selfish action contrary to the Covenant;

and no state is powerful enough to stand for long against the League if the governments in the League and their peoples are determined that the Covenant shall be upheld.

At the League of Nations in Geneva speaking as President of the Council and Acting President of the Assembly, 26 September 1932.

Despite our juridical equality here, in matters such as European peace the small states are powerless. As I have already said, peace is dependent upon the will of the great states. All the small states can do, if the statesmen of the greater states fail in their duty, is resolutely to determine that they will not become the tools of any great power and that they will resist with whatever strength they may possess every attempt to force them into a war against their will.

At the League of Nations Asembly in Geneva, 2 July 1936

The war of sheer aggression, the war of the bully who covets what does not belong to him and means to possess himself of it by force, is not the war that we need fear most. The most dangerous war is that which has its origin in just claims denied or in a clash of opposing rights — and not merely opposing interests — when each side can see no reason in justice why it should yield its claims to the other. If, by conceding the claims of justice or by reasonable compromise in a spirit of fair play, we take steps to avoid the latter kind of war, we can face the possibility of the other kind with relative equanimity. Despite certain preaching, mankind *has* advanced, and the public conscience, in a clear case of aggression, will count and may well be, in a European war, a decisive factor.

As President of the Assembly of the League of Nations on radio from Geneva, 25 September 1938

Let us begin by endeavouring to make a League of Nations effective for Europe, and it will quickly become applicable to the world. Until the soul of Europe is at peace, there cannot be real peace or co-operation anywhere else.

Ibid.

A small nation has to be extremely cautious when it enters into alliances which bring it, willy-nilly, into those wars. As I said during the last war, the position was that we would not be consulted in how war would be started — the great powers would do that — and when it was ended, no matter who won, suppose the side on which we were won, we would not be consulted as to the terms on which it should end.

Dáil Éireann, 12 July 1955

14. The Partition of Ireland

. . . a regard for justice in the matter of the north-east settlement would have given Ireland internal peace. But in selecting an arbitary area of six counties for the Northern State, in defiance of the desires of the majorities in several areas within these counties, justice was flouted and injustice, as usual, has been compelled to maintain itself by force.

Statement on the assassination of Field Marshal Sir Henry Wilson,
23 June 1922

Ireland is more than a political union of states. It has been a nation from the dawn of history, united in traditions, in political institutions, in territory. The island is too small to be divided; it does not need and cannot afford two governments, with all the duplication of services and expenses which that involves. The pretext that partition was necessary to save a minority of Irishmen from religious persecution at the hands of the majority was an invention without any basis in the facts of our time or in the history of the past. No nation respects the rights of conscience more than Ireland, whose people too long bore persecution themselves to desire to inflict it on others. But British policy was not even consistent with the pretext invented to justify it; on the plea of saving one religious minority, it created two; on the plea of protecting the rights of a powerful and well-organised Protestant minority of twenty-five per cent, it split that minority, leaving part of it as a helpless remnant scattered through twenty-six counties.

Partition has no political or economic justification.

Broadcast to United States on Lincoln's birthday, 12 February 1933

There is no use in pretending that we can solve that by mere words. We cannot; nor can we solve it by force. We have got to solve it, as I have said, in the only way it can be solved, and that is by having a livelihood for our people down here which will be the envy of the people in the North and make them see that their future lies with their own people and not with strangers. There are old prejudices that die hard. — They are dying very hard in the North, but they are dying, please God, and the people of this country will yet — I cannot say when, I am not a prophet, but this I am certain of — the nation that for seven hundred years resisted all the power that could be brought against it, that nation is going to continue till it sees a united nation, but the part that we can effectively rule that we rule it in such a way that our citizens will be proud of it.

Address to Fianna Fáil Ard Fheis, 8 November 1933

15. Religion

The Irish question is fundamentally and entirely a political struggle between Ireland and Britain — between Irish nationality and British imperialism. That it is not a religious struggle can be seen from the fact that Catholic Ireland fought Catholic England centuries before Martin Luther nailed up his theses. Protestant Ireland fought Protestant England. Some of the bitterest opponents of Irish freedom today are Catholic Englishmen. Irish Protestants and Irish Catholics alike have suffered death for Irish liberty. The struggle for the Republic was initiated by Protestants, and in the past century and a half the foremost Irish leaders have been Protestants — Wolfe Tone, Russell, McCracken, Orr, Lord Edward Fitzgerald, Robert Emmet, John Mitchel, Thomas Davis, Smith O'Brien, down to Butt and Parnell. It is obvious that, if the Irish cause had been a religious cause, the majority would not have chosen their leaders from the creed they were supposed to be opposing. This alone disproves the pretence that the Irish struggle against England is founded in a rivalry of religious beliefs.

Message to President Wilson of the United States, 27 October 1920

The existing partition is based fundamentally on party-political differences. Party politics in Britain originated it, and similar politics keep it alive today.

Certain factors give partition a religious complexion, but the division is not based on religion.

Interview with the Evening Standard *of London, 13 October 1938*

Certain representations have been made to me.

I have made no public statement because I have clung to the hope that good sense and decent neighbourly feeling would of themselves bring this business to an end. I cannot say that I know every fact, but if, as head of the government, I must speak, I can only say, from what has appeared in public, that I regard this boycott as ill-conceived, ill-considered, and futile for the achievement of the purpose for which it seems to have been intended; that I regard it as unjust and cruel to confound the innocent with the guilty; that I repudiate any suggestion that this boycott is typical of the attitude or conduct of our people; that I am convinced that ninety per cent of them look on this matter as I do; and that I beg of all who have regard for the fair name, good repute and well-being of our nation to use their influence to bring this deplorable affair to a speedy end.

Dáil Éireann. On boycott of Protestants in Fethard-on-Sea, Co. Wexford, 4 July 1957

16. Republicanism

I stand definitely for the Irish Republic as it was established — as it was proclaimed in 1916 — as it was constitutionally established by the Irish nation in 1919, and I stand for that definitely; and I will stand by no policy whatever that is not consistent with that.

Dáil Éireann, 6 January 1922

Republicans, you have come here today to the tomb of Wolfe Tone on a pilgrimage of loyalty! By your presence you proclaim your undiminished attachment to the ideals of Tone, and your unaltered devotion to the cause for which he gave his life. It is your answer to those who would have it believed that the Republic of Ireland is dead and its cause abandoned.

Republicans — you who were privileged to repeat your vows at this shrine in the company of Clarke and Pearse and Connolly, of Cathal Brugha and Liam Mellows — you who were admitted to the comradeship of heroes, and have drunk of the same draughts of freedom, and caught the same glimpses of the Land of Promise, you are not here in hypocrisy or in an idle demonstration of a lifeless faith! You are here to bear witness to that which is living and true — immortal and secure above every chance of fortune — to the aspirations of the Irish people for freedom, and you are here to pledge your sincerity and your constancy, your toil and your sacrifice, until these aspirations be achieved.

Yes, the achievement of these aspirations to the full — that is the task which you, Republicans, have consciously set yourselves.

At the grave of Wolfe Tone at Bodenstown, 21 June 1925

There has been a wrong interpretation put on our history over the past forty years. They tell you that we who were in the Republican army were acting as they are acting. That is not true. In 1918 there was an election here, from which was elected a government — an election which gave a vast majority in favour of the programme that was set. When I went to America, I went there as the head of the elected government of the Irish Republic. I was elected, and every action of the Republican army was taken as an action of the army authorised by the government of the Republic.

We were not self-appointed. We were elected, and it was as the elected government that the army of the Republic fought from 1919 to 1921. They talk about the Civil War and say, 'Oh yes, you went into a civil war and you don't care about the people's will.' I say we did. We were the regulars of that time. We fought to maintain the Republic that was set up by the Irish people, that the representatives of the Irish people were sent to Dáil Éireann to uphold the Republic that they swore to uphold.

Our position was that the representatives were elected to maintain the Republic and that they had no right to turn down the Republic without the people's will. In the Pact Election they said we wanted civil war. We did not; we did everything in our power to prevent it. The new Dáil was to meet within two days after the time in which the Four Courts were attacked. It wasn't we who forced the Civil War. It was they who didn't allow Dáil Éireann to meet.

Fianna Fáil Ard Fheis, 19 November 1957

Is cuimhin leis na daoine a bhí beo an t-am sin gur cuireadh deireadh leis an gCogadh Mór i mí na Samhna 1918. An mhí ina dhiaidh sin, mí na Nollag, bhí olltoghchán anseo. Bhain Sinn Féin feidhm as an olltoghchán sin ionas go mbeadh eolas ag an domhan uile gurbh í mian mhuintir na hÉireann a bheith saor, neamhspleách. I rith an chogaidh duirt ceannairí Mheiriceá agus Shasana gurbh é faoi deara an troid a bhí ar siúl ná cearta na náisiún beag a chosaint agus a chaomhnú. Toradh an olltoghcháin anseo, níor fhág sé aon amhras céard ba mhian le muintir na hÉireann — gurbh í a mian a bheith saor, neamhspleách, agus poblacht mar chóras rialtais acu.

De na daoine a tháinig le chéile an uair sin, tá seisear beo fós, seisear de lucht na Dála; agus tá seisear beo freisin de na daoine a bhí as láthair. Tar éis an toghcháin seoladh cuireadh chuig na Teachtaí a bhí tofa. Dhá thrian ar a laghad, díobh sin, de mhuintir Sinn Féin iad. Tháinig anseo na Teachtaí a bhain le Sinn Féin, na daoine a bhí saor chuige. Níor fhéad a lán acu, an chuid is mó díobh, níor fhéad siad a bheith

86

anseo: bhíodar i ngéibheann i Sasana, nó ar díbirt nó ag déanamh oibre eile ar son an náisiúin.

Ach ar an méad a tháinig anseo bhí Cathal Brugha i gceannas, agus tar éis na paidre adúirt an tAthair Ó Flanagáin sheas Cathal Brugha agus léigh sé amach an Fháisnéis Neamhspleáchais; labhair seisean as Gaeilge. Léigh daoine eile ansin an rud céanna as Fraincís agus as Béarla. Chuir sé sin in iúl don domhan mór gurbh í ár mian a bheith saor, neamhspleách agus gur poblacht a bheadh mar chóras rialtais againn.

Óráid don Dáil agus don tSeanaid — 40 bliain tar éis bunú
Dáil Éireann, 21 Eanáir 1969

An t-am sin, bhí mórán de mhuintir Sinn Féin sna hÓglaigh chomh maith, agus cé gurbh dhá eagraíocht ar leith iad Sinn Féin agus na hÓglaigh, d'oibríodar as lámha a chéile chomh dlúth sin go gceapfadh aon duine nach raibh ann ach aon eagraíocht amháin. Bhí díograis i gcroí gach aon duine acu, agus nuair a thángadar anseo bhí fúthu na rudaí a bhí in aigne ár ndaoine a dhéanamh chomh tapaidh agus ab fhéidir.

Ní hamháin gur chuireadar ráiteas amach, mar adúirt mé, go mba mhian linn a bheith saor, neamhspleách, ach chuireadar Teachtaireacht chomh maith chuig Saor-Náisiúin an Domhain ag iarraidh orthu aitheantas a thabhairt don Phoblacht. Léadh amach freisin clár ina raibh aidhmeanna Sinn Féin ag an uair sin, aidhmeanna comhdhaonnacha agus eacnamaíochta. Bhí obair an lae sin críochnaithe go maith ansin.

Ibid.

Tá daoine ann faoi láthair agus ceapann siad go bhfuil smaointe agus aidhmeanna an náisiúnachais a bhí ag na treoraithe leathchéad bliain ó shin, go bhfuil siad sin sean-aimseartha inniu agus as dáta. Tá a lán cainte faoi iltíreachas agus mar sin, agus tá daoine a cheapann nach bhfuil i ndán do na náisiúin bheaga anois ach a bheith brúite i leataobh nó báite nó súite isteach i gcumhachtaí móra. Ní hí sin mo thuairimse ar chor ar bith. Ba cheart muinín níos mó a bheith againne go mairfidh an náisiún seo ná mar a bhí ag daoine leathchéad bliain ó shin. Ceannairí Sheachtain na Cásca, cheapadarsan go gcinnteodh an tÉirí Amach go mairfeadh an náisiún seo. Tá sé sin le léamh as an litir dheireannach a chuir Seán Mac Diarmada ó Chill Mhaighneann an lá sular cuireadh chun báis é.

Ba cheart, mar adúirt mé, níos mó muiníne a bheith againn anois go mairfidh ár náisiún ná mar a bhí ag an am sin. Ní cheaptar gur cúige sinn anois: tá a fhios ag an saol mór gur náisiún sinn. Táimid ag glacadh ár náite i measc na náisiún agus ag oibriú leo chun leasa an chine dhaonna ar fad a chur ar aghaidh.

Ibid.

EAMON DE VALERA
14 October 1882 – 29 August 1975

1882 Born in New York, the son of Vivion Juan de Valera of Seville, Spain, and Catherine Coll of Knockmore, Bruree, Co Limerick, Ireland.

1885 Vivion de Valera died leaving his widow and child in poor circumstances. Eamon taken to Ireland by his Uncle Ned. There he was entrusted to the care of his grandmother Elizabeth Coll, her son Patrick and her daughter Hannie.

1888 Started his education at Bruree National School.

1896 Grandmother died. Patrick Coll effectively became Eamon's guardian.

1896-1901 At Christian Brothers' School in Charleville, Co Cork, and later at Blackrock College, Co Dublin.

1904 Was granted a B.A. degree by the Royal University of Ireland and later began work as a teacher of mathematics.

1906-1907 Studied at Trinity College, Dublin.

1908 Joined the Gaelic League and began a life-long interest in the Irish language and the cause of restoration.

1910 Married Sinéad Ní Fhlanagáin, his Irish teacher.

1913 Joined the Irish Volunteers at the first public meeting held by that organisation.

1916 Served as a Commandant in the Easter Week Insurrection, was the last Commandant to surrender, was sentenced to death but was reprieved and sentenced to imprisonment for life. His American birth and the intervention, at Mrs de Valera's request, of Edward L. Adams, United States Consul at Dublin, would appear to have saved his life.

1917 General Amnesty for Republican prisoners. Elected

MP for East Clare in by-election standing for demands and claims made in the 1916 Insurrection. Accepted widely, because of his 1916 record, as the natural leader of Republican Ireland. Elected President of Sinn Féin in succession to Arthur Griffith, the Sinn Féin founder, and also President of the Irish Volunteers, by now often referred to as the Irish Republican Army (IRA).

1918 Took leading part in campaign to resist conscription of Irishmen into British army. Arrested and jailed in England for alleged complicity in a plot with the German Empire. Re-elected for Clare in general election in which Sinn Féin became the country's leading party.

1919 Following his escape from jail in England de Valera was elected Príomh Aire (Premier) by the revolutionary Dáil Éireann on 1 April. Some weeks later he travelled in secret to the United States where he remained until the end of 1920 publicising the Irish Republic and the war against English rule in Ireland, collecting funds for Dáil Éireann and seeking support for the Irish cause from political and powerful factions.

1921 Involved in many efforts to end the war honourably. Following the Truce of 11 July between the Irish Republican Army and the British army, de Valera, Griffith and others travelled to London for talks with the British government. In the event these talks involved only de Valera and the British Prime Minister, David Lloyd George, and took place in July and early August. No agreement was reached. The British would allow a certain form of colonial home rule to twenty-six of the thirty-two Irish counties, would not tolerate the idea of a free Irish State of any sort, let alone a Republic, and did not envisage the Six Counties of North-East Ulster as being part of the Irish State. Later another Irish delegation led by Arthur Giffith and Michael Collins negotiated in London with Mr Lloyd George and his ministers.

They agreed to an arrangement giving greater freedom than that earlier suggested by the British but excluding the Six Counties and including the English King as King of Ireland, the new Irish Free State to be part of the British Empire and Commonwealth. De Valera rejected this agreement. De Valera elected Chancellor of the National University of Ireland.

1922 Following a most bitter debate which divided nationalist Ireland, Dáil Éireann by a small majority agreed to the London settlement. De Valera resigned as head of the Republican government and Arthur Griffith took his place. The work of dismantling the Republic and establishing the Free State began. Griffith was in charge of the Dáil Éireann government and Michael Collins of the Free State 'Provisional Government'; they worked hand in glove for a time. IRA leaders, shocked at what the politicians had done, repudiated all of them and under the leadership of Rory O'Connor, declared themselves an independent entity. Clashes occurred between troops of the Free State and IRA volunteers.

Following the assassination in London of Field Marshal Sir Henry Wilson, the British government insisted that the Free State government should end the activities of the IRA or, if not, the British army would do so. The Free State government complied, attacked the Fourt Courts where Rory O'Connor had his headquarters, and so started a countrywide Civil War. De Valera had already been pushed aside by the militant Republicans but joined with them as an ordinary rank and file volunteer when they were attacked. The Civil War was especially vicious but with the support of the clergy of all denominations, the newspapers and the moneyed people, as well as that of the British government, the Free State eventually won conclusively.

1923 As Republican resistance crumbled, de Valera was called back to find some honorable way out. But the

Free Staters would not deal with him and on 24 May Frank Aiken, the IRA chief-of-staff, called a cease-fire and de Valera issued a message to Republicans suggesting that other ways must now be attempted to save the Republic. He was later arrested by Free State soldiers and kept in jail for months without trial.

1924 Released from jail. Republican movement at its lowest.

1925 IRA no longer satisfied with de Valera; took the attitude it should not be answerable to political authority. Free State acknowledged Six County State there by right and gave it its legal recognition. Sinn Féin deputies who boycotted Dáil Éireann because of the Oath of Allegiance to the English King, could only denounce this action in impotent fashion.

1926 Sinn Féin turned down suggestion by de Valera that if the Oath of Allegiance were removed from Free State Dáil, Republican deputies could then take their seats with honour. De Valera and likeminded people formed Fianna Fáil, a new Republican party intent on winning power by the ballot paper in the Free State and changing it from the inside.

1927 Following an election and after the assassination of Kevin O'Higgins, Vice-President of the Executive Council of the Free State, Eamon de Valera led Fianna Fáil into the Free State Dáil. He described the Oath of Allegiance as an empty formality.

1931 He founded *The Irish Press* to ensure that people could learn of Fianna Fáil's nationalist and republican policies and programmes.

1932 Fianna Fáil led by de Valera formed Free State government following election in which Fianna Fáil became largest party. De Valera elected President of the Executive Council and Minister for External Affairs. Began process which abolished Oath of Allegiance; ended payment of land annuities; became President of the Council and Acting President of the Assembly of the League of Nations. After public differences with the Governor General, James MacNeill, de Valera insisted on his removal from office.

1933 Fianna Fáil under de Valera won overall majority in January elections. Dismissed Garda Commissioner Eoin O'Duffy. Acted against the Blueshirts, a fascist organisation directed by former Free State ministers and led by General O'Duffy.

1936 De Valera abolished University Representation in Dáil Éireann. Later abolished Seanad Éireann. On abdication of Edward VIII of England, introduced External Relations Bill which recognised the English King as being empowered to act for the Free State in certain diplomatic matters but removed all other references to the King from the Free State constitution.

1937 Introduced new constitution which the people later enacted by referendum. Offices of President of Ireland, Taoiseach and Tanaiste created.

1938 Successful negotiations with the British on the 'Economic War' which Britain had initiated in 1932 over the non-payment of land annuities. Treaty ports which British held since 1922 returned to Irish control. De Valera President of the Assembly of the League of Nations.

1939 De Valera declared that in a future war Ireland would be neutral. De Valera through Neville Chamberlain ensured that British conscription would not be extended to the Six Counties. IRA outlawed and many of its members interned without trial. De Valera appointed himself Minister for Education.

1940 De Valera rejected British promise on Irish unity in return for Irish participation in war. Established the Dublin Institute for Advanced Studies.

1941 Refused to meet Winston Churchill in person.

1942 Protested against American troop landings in the Six Counties.

1943 Emerged from general election without overall majority but managed to form government.

1944 Rejected ultimatum from American and British governments to expel German, Italian and Japanese diplomats from Ireland. Won general election.

1948 After sixteen years in power defeated in general election and replaced by John A. Costello who headed an Inter-Party government. Began an anti-Partition campaign in the United States, Australia and India.

1949 The Twenty-six County State became 'The Republic of Ireland'. De Valera regarded this as an ill-advised move.

1951 After the fall of the Inter-Party government de Valera once again became Taoiseach.

1954 Defeated again in elections, he became Leader of the Opposition.

1957 De Valera won his greatest majority ever on 20 March when Fianna Fáil took 78 of the 147 Dáil seats. Among first acts of new government was the re-introduction of internment without trial for IRA volunteers involved in a new campaign in the Six Counties.

1959 In June defeated in major attempt to persuade electorate to abolish the proportional representation system of voting and bring back the British first-past-the-post system. Elected President of Ireland.

1966 Re-elected President.

1973 On his last day in office as President addressed a public meeting at Boland's Mills, his 1916 headquarters, in which he said he believed Irish unity would be achieved in the not-too-distant future.

1975 Died on 29 August, his wife Sinéad having died on 7 January.

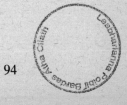

DE VALERA'S DARKEST HOUR 1919-1932
T. Ryle Dwyer

De Valera's Darkest Hour is the story of Eamon de Valera's struggle for national independence during the most controversial period of his career. It deals with his election as Priomh Aire of Dail Eireann, his unauthorised assumption of the title of President, his controversial tour of the United States, his obscure part in the negotiations leading to the Anglo-Irish Treaty and his reasons for rejecting the Treaty. De Valera's misunderstood role in the period leading up to and during the Civil War, and finally his spectacular recovery in lifting himself from the despised depths of 1923 to become President of the Executive Council of the Irish Free State in less than nine years are covered in detail.

DE VALERA'S FINEST HOUR 1932-1959
T. Ryle Dwyer

Throughout his long career de Valera was a controversial figure but even his greatest critics give him credit both for his courageous denunciation of international aggression during the 1930s and for his adroit diplomatic skill in keeping Ireland out of the Second World War in the face of Nazi provocation and intense Allied pressure. His policy was guided by one paramount consideration — his concept of the best interests of the Irish people. He pursued those interests with such determination that he became the virtual personification of Irish independence.

Dr. Dwyer gives a graphic account of de Valera's quest for national independence. Of particular interest are well-chosen and carefully documented extracts from contemporary letters, speeches, newspaper articles, etc., giving many new insights into the thoughts and motives of this enigmatic politician, who has left an indelible imprint on Irish history.

MICHAEL COLLINS AND THE TREATY
His Differences with de Valera
T. Ryle Dwyer

To Michael Collins the signing of the Treaty between Ireland and Britain in 1921 was a 'Stepping Stone'. Eamon de Valera called it 'Treason'.

The controversy surrounding this Treaty is probably the single most important factor in the history of this country, not only because it led to the Civil War of 1922-1923 but also because the basic differences between the country's two main political parties stem from the dispute.

T. Ryle Dwyer not only takes an in-depth look at the characters and motivations of the two main Irish protagonists but also gives many insights into the views and ideas of the other people involved on both sides of the Irish Sea.

This book is not only the story of Michael Collins' role in the events surrounding the Treaty, but it is also the story of his differences with Eamon de Valera which were to have tragic consequences for the nation.

BROTHER AGAINST BROTHER
Liam Deasy

Brother against Brother is Liam Deasy's moving and sensitive account of the Civil War — Ireland's greatest tragedy.

He tells in detail of the Republican disillusionment with the Truce, and later with the Treaty; how the Civil War began; how the Republicans were hopelessly outnumbered and hunted in the hills like wild animals before they were finally broken and defeated.

For the first time Liam Deasy recalls the circumstances surrounding his much criticised order appealing to his comrades to call off the Civil War — an order which saved the lives of hundreds of prisoners.

In a special chapter he recounts his involvement in the ambush at Bealnablath where his close friend, Michael Collins, met his death.

Liam Deasy was one of the greatest military leaders thrown up by the Revolution and he writes without bitterness or malice, but with humility and understanding towards all. He gives us a rare and profound insight into the brutal, suicidal war that set father against son and brother against brother.

QUOTATIONS FROM P. H. PEARSE
Compiled and Introduced by
Proinsias Mac Aonghusa

Patrick Henry Pearse has had more influence on Ireland of the twentieth century than any other person. The very fact that, sixty years and more after his execution by an English firing squad, some men should spend time and energy devising ways to denigrate him speaks for itself.

This book, with a Preface by Sean MacBride, may serve for some as an introduction to the writings of Pearse and for others as an opportunity to sample the range and depth of his writings.

ONE DAY IN BY LIFE
Bobby Sands

One Day in My Life is a human document of suffering, determination, anguish, courage and faith. It also portrays frightening examples of man's inhumanity to man.

Written with economy and a dry humour it charts, almost minute by minute, a brave man's struggle to preserve his identity against cold, dirt and boredom. It is the record of a single day and conjures up vividly the enclosed hell of Long Kesh; the poor food, the harassment and the humiliating mirror searches. Bobby Sands and his comrades were often gripped by terror at the iron system that held them and yet their courage never faltered.

Written on toilet paper with a biro refill and hidden inside Bobby Sands' own body, this is a book about human bravery and endurance and will take its place beside the great European classics on imprisonment like *One Day in the Life of Ivan Denisovich* and our own John Mitchel's *Jail Journal.*

'I wish it were possible to ensure that those in charge of formulating British policy in Ireland would read these pages. They might begin to understand the deep injuries which British policy has inflicted upon this nation, and now seek to heal these wounds.' *From the Introduction by Sean MacBride.*

Bobby Sands was twenty-seven years old when he died, on the sixty-sixth day of his hunger-strike, on 5 May 1981. He had spent almost the last nine years of his short life in prison because of his Irish Republican activities. By the time of his death he was world famous for having embarrassed the British establishment by being elected as M.P. to the British Parliament for Fermanagh/South Tyrone and having defiantly withstood political and moral pressure to abandon his hunger-strike.